Title:

"Deep Seek: Unraveling the Mysteries of AI's New Frontier"

Table of Contents:

Introduction: The Quest for Intelligence

Overview: Introduce the concept of artificial intelligence (AI) and its evolution over the years. Highlight the significance of the Deep Seek model as a groundbreaking development in AI research.

Objective: Explain the purpose of the book—to demystify the Deep Seek model and its algorithms for both technical and non-technical readers.

Tone: Set a tone of curiosity and wonder, comparing the journey of understanding Deep Seek to exploring a new world.

CHAPTER 1: THE BIRTH OF DEEP SEEK – A NEW ERA IN AI

Content: Discuss the origins of the Deep Seek model, its inspiration from biological systems, and how it differs from traditional AI models.

Analogy: Compare the development of Deep Seek to the invention of the telescope, which opened up new realms of exploration.

Scenario: Imagine a world where machines can "think" like humans, and introduce Deep Seek as the key to unlocking this potential.

CHAPTER 2: THE BUILDING BLOCKS OF DEEP SEEK – NEURONS AND NETWORKS

Content: Explain the basic components of the Deep Seek model, such as artificial neurons and neural networks.

Analogy: Relate artificial neurons to the neurons in the human brain, and neural networks to a team of experts working together to solve a problem.

Scenario: Use a real-life example, like recognizing faces in a crowd, to illustrate how neural networks function.

CHAPTER 3: THE ALGORITHMIC HEARTBEAT – HOW DEEP SEEK LEARNS

Content: Dive into the core algorithms that power Deep Seek, including backpropagation and gradient descent.

Analogy: Compare the learning process of Deep Seek to a student learning from mistakes and improving over time.

Scenario: Describe a scenario where Deep Seek learns to play a game, gradually improving its strategy through trial and error.

CHAPTER 4: THE POWER OF DATA – FUELING DEEP SEEK'S INTELLIGENCE

Content: Discuss the role of data in training the Deep Seek model, including data collection, preprocessing, and augmentation.

Analogy: Compare data to the food that fuels the brain, emphasizing the importance of quality and quantity.

Scenario: Use the example of a self-driving car learning to navigate through different environments by analyzing vast amounts of data.

CHAPTER 5: THE ART OF TRAINING – TEACHING DEEP SEEK TO THINK

Content: Explain the training process, including epochs, batches, and loss functions.

Analogy: Relate training Deep Seek to teaching a child to ride a bike, with each attempt bringing them closer to mastery.

Scenario: Illustrate the training process with a story of Deep Seek learning to recognize different species of flowers.

CHAPTER 6: THE MAGIC OF LAYERS – DEEP LEARNING IN ACTION

Content: Explore the concept of deep learning and the role of multiple layers in the Deep Seek model.

Analogy: Compare the layers of the model to the layers of an onion, each revealing a deeper level of understanding.

Scenario: Use the example of Deep Seek analyzing a complex image, such as a cityscape, to show how each layer extracts different features.

CHAPTER 7: THE VISION OF DEEP SEEK – SEEING THE WORLD THROUGH AI EYES

Content: Discuss how Deep Seek processes visual information, including convolutional neural networks (CNNs).

Analogy: Compare CNNs to the human visual system, where different parts of the brain recognize different aspects of an image.

Scenario: Describe how Deep Seek can identify objects in a photo, such as distinguishing between a cat and a dog.

CHAPTER 8:
THE LANGUAGE
OF MACHINES
– DEEP SEEK'S
UNDERSTANDING
OF TEXT

Content: Explain how Deep Seek processes and understands text, including natural language processing (NLP) techniques.

Analogy: Relate NLP to learning a new language, where Deep Seek must understand grammar, context, and meaning.

Scenario: Use the example of Deep Seek translating a sentence from one language to another, capturing the nuances of meaning.

CHAPTER 9:
THE SOUND OF INTELLIGENCE – DEEP SEEK'S AUDITORY SKILLS

Content: Explore how Deep Seek processes audio data, including speech recognition and sound analysis.

Analogy: Compare Deep Seek's auditory processing to a musician learning to play by ear, recognizing patterns and melodies.

Scenario: Describe a scenario where Deep Seek transcribes a spoken conversation, accurately capturing every word.

CHAPTER 10: THE DECISION-MAKER – DEEP SEEK'S ROLE IN PROBLEM SOLVING

Content: Discuss how Deep Seek makes decisions, including reinforcement learning and decision trees.

Analogy: Compare Deep Seek's decision-making process to a chess player strategizing their next move.

Scenario: Illustrate with an example of Deep Seek playing a game of chess, learning from each move to improve its strategy.

CHAPTER 11: THE ETHICAL COMPASS – NAVIGATING THE MORAL LANDSCAPE OF AI

Content: Address the ethical considerations of using Deep Seek, including bias, privacy, and accountability.

Analogy: Compare the ethical challenges of AI to navigating a ship through a storm, requiring careful guidance and responsibility.

Scenario: Discuss a hypothetical situation where Deep Seek is used in a sensitive application, such as hiring, and the ethical dilemmas that arise.

CHAPTER 12: THE FUTURE OF DEEP SEEK – BEYOND THE HORIZON

Content: Speculate on the future developments of Deep Seek and its potential impact on society.

Analogy: Compare the future of Deep Seek to the exploration of space, with endless possibilities and unknown frontiers.

Scenario: Imagine a future where Deep Seek is integrated into everyday life, from healthcare to education, transforming the way we live.

CHAPTER 13: THE HUMAN-AI PARTNERSHIP – COLLABORATING WITH DEEP SEEK

Content: Explore the concept of human-AI collaboration, where Deep Seek works alongside humans to achieve common goals.

Analogy: Compare the partnership to a symphony orchestra, where each member contributes their unique skills to create harmony.

Scenario: Describe a scenario where Deep Seek assists a doctor in diagnosing a rare disease, combining human intuition with AI's analytical power.

CHAPTER 14: THE CHALLENGES AHEAD – OVERCOMING OBSTACLES IN AI DEVELOPMENT

Content: Discuss the challenges faced in developing and deploying Deep Seek, including technical limitations and societal resistance.

Analogy: Compare the challenges to climbing a mountain, where each step brings new obstacles but also new vistas.

Scenario: Use the example of Deep Seek being deployed in a disaster zone, highlighting the difficulties and rewards of using AI in critical situations.

CHAPTER 15: THE LEGACY OF DEEP SEEK – SHAPING THE FUTURE OF INTELLIGENCE

Content: Reflect on the impact of Deep Seek on the field of AI and its potential to shape the future of intelligence.

Analogy: Compare the legacy of Deep Seek to the invention of the printing press, which revolutionized the way knowledge is shared.

Scenario: Conclude with a vision of a world where Deep Seek has become an integral part of society, enhancing human capabilities and driving progress.

Conclusion: The Journey Continues

Content: Summarize the key takeaways from the book and encourage readers to continue exploring the fascinating world of AI.

Tone: End on an inspiring note, emphasizing that the journey of understanding and developing AI is just beginning.

Call to Action: Invite readers to engage with AI in their own lives, whether through learning, experimentation, or simply staying curious.

Appendices:

Glossary of Terms: Define key AI and Deep Seek terms in simple language.

Further Reading: Provide a list of resources for readers who want to dive deeper into the subject.

Interactive Elements: Include QR codes or links to online simulations and tools where readers can experiment with AI concepts.

Design and Layout:

Visuals: Use diagrams, illustrations, and infographics to explain complex concepts.

Sidebars: Include interesting facts, historical anecdotes, and real-world examples in sidebars to keep readers engaged.

Interactive Questions: Pose thought-provoking questions at the end of each chapter to encourage reflection and discussion.

This book is designed to be a comprehensive yet accessible guide to the Deep Seek model, blending technical depth with engaging storytelling to captivate readers from all backgrounds.

Introduction: The Quest for Intelligence

Imagine a world where machines can think, learn, and even

dream. A world where artificial intelligence (AI) doesn't just mimic human behavior but understands it, adapts to it, and evolves alongside it. This is not the plot of a science fiction novel —it's the reality we're stepping into, thanks to groundbreaking advancements like the Deep Seek model.

Welcome to the beginning of a journey—a quest to unravel the mysteries of intelligence, both human and artificial. This book is your guide to understanding how the Deep Seek model works, why it's revolutionary, and how it's shaping the future of AI. Whether you're a seasoned AI researcher or someone who's never written a line of code, this book is designed to demystify the complexities of Deep Seek and make its wonders accessible to everyone.

The Evolution of Intelligence: From Humans to Machines

Intelligence is one of the most fascinating phenomena in the universe. For millennia, humans have been the sole bearers of this gift, using it to build civilizations, create art, and explore the cosmos. But what if intelligence isn't exclusive to humans? What if we could create machines that not only replicate our cognitive abilities but also surpass them?

This is the question that has driven the field of artificial intelligence since its inception. The journey of AI began in the 1950s, when pioneers like Alan Turing asked, "Can machines think?" Back then, computers were rudimentary, and the idea of machine intelligence was more philosophical than practical. But as technology advanced, so did our ambitions.

In the 1980s, the rise of neural networks—computational

models inspired by the human brain—marked a turning point. These networks could learn from data, recognize patterns, and make decisions. However, they were limited by the technology of the time. Fast forward to the 21st century, and we've entered the era of deep learning, where AI systems can process vast amounts of data, understand natural language, and even beat world champions at games like chess and Go.

But the story doesn't end there. The Deep Seek model represents the next leap in this evolution—a model that doesn't just learn from data but seeks understanding, much like a curious human mind.

What is Deep Seek? A New Frontier in AI

At its core, Deep Seek is a deep learning model—a type of AI that uses layers of artificial neurons to process information. But what sets Deep Seek apart is its ability to actively seek out knowledge. Traditional AI models are passive; they wait for data to be fed to them. Deep Seek, on the other hand, is proactive. It explores, questions, and connects ideas in ways that were previously thought impossible for machines.

Think of Deep Seek as a detective. Imagine you're trying to solve a mystery. A traditional AI might wait for you to provide all the clues before making a guess. But Deep Seek doesn't wait—it goes out, gathers clues, forms hypotheses, and refines its understanding until it cracks the case. This ability to seek knowledge is what makes Deep Seek so powerful—and so intriguing.

Why Deep Seek Matters: The Promise of AI

The Deep Seek model isn't just a technical achievement; it's a paradigm shift in how we think about AI. Here's why it matters:

Deeper Understanding: Deep Seek doesn't just recognize patterns; it understands context. For example, it can read a sentence and grasp not just the words but the meaning behind them.

Adaptability: Unlike traditional models that are rigid and specialized, Deep Seek can adapt to new tasks and environments. It's like a Swiss Army knife of AI—versatile and always ready to learn.

Human-Like Reasoning: Deep Seek's algorithms are designed to mimic human thought processes, making it more intuitive and relatable. This opens up new possibilities for collaboration between humans and machines.

Real-World Applications: From healthcare to education, Deep Seek has the potential to revolutionize industries. Imagine a doctor using Deep Seek to diagnose diseases with unprecedented accuracy or a teacher using it to personalize lessons for every student.

The Purpose of This Book: Demystifying Deep Seek

The world of AI can seem intimidating, filled

with jargon and complex concepts. Terms like neural networks, backpropagation, and gradient descent might sound like they belong in a science lab, not in everyday conversation. But here's the truth: you don't need to be a computer scientist to understand Deep Seek.

This book is designed to break down the Deep Seek model into simple, relatable concepts. We'll use analogies, real-world examples, and engaging scenarios to explain how Deep Seek works and why it's such a big deal. By the end of this journey, you'll not only understand Deep Seek—you'll see the world of AI in a whole new light.

The Journey Ahead: Exploring Deep Seek

To help you navigate this exploration, the book is divided into 15 chapters, each focusing on a different aspect of Deep Seek. Here's a sneak peek at what's to come:

The Birth of Deep Seek: Discover the origins of this revolutionary model and how it builds on decades of AI research.

The Building Blocks of Deep Seek: Learn about the artificial neurons and networks that form the foundation of Deep Seek.

The Algorithmic Heartbeat: Dive into the algorithms that power Deep Seek's learning process.

The Power of Data: Explore how data fuels Deep Seek's intelligence and why quality matters.

The Art of Training: Understand how Deep Seek learns from its mistakes and improves over time.

The Magic of Layers: Uncover the role of deep learning in making Deep Seek so powerful.

The Vision of Deep Seek: See how Deep Seek processes visual information, from images to videos.

The Language of Machines: Learn how Deep Seek understands and generates human language.

The Sound of Intelligence: Discover how Deep Seek processes audio data, from speech to music.

The Decision-Maker: Explore how Deep Seek makes decisions and solves problems.

The Ethical Compass: Discuss the ethical challenges of using Deep Seek and how to address them.

The Future of Deep Seek: Imagine the possibilities of Deep Seek in the years to come.

The Human-AI Partnership: See how Deep Seek can collaborate with humans to achieve common goals.

The Challenges Ahead: Acknowledge the obstacles in developing and deploying Deep Seek.

The Legacy of Deep Seek: Reflect on the impact of Deep Seek and its role in shaping the future of intelligence.

A World of Wonder Awaits

As you turn the pages of this book, you'll embark on a journey that's both enlightening and exhilarating. You'll meet the pioneers who laid the groundwork for Deep Seek, explore the algorithms that make it tick, and imagine the future it's helping to create. Along the way, you'll encounter stories, analogies, and examples that bring the world of AI to life.

So, whether you're a curious reader, a student, or a professional looking to expand your horizons, this book is for you. The quest for intelligence is one of the most exciting adventures of our time—and Deep Seek is leading the way. Are you ready to join the journey?

Let's begin.

A Glimpse of What's to Come

To give you a taste of the journey ahead, here's a short scenario that illustrates the power of Deep Seek:

Scenario: The Curious Detective

Imagine you're a detective trying to solve a complex case. You have a mountain of evidence—photos, witness statements, and forensic reports—but no clear leads. Enter Deep Seek, your AI assistant.

Instead of waiting for you to analyze the data, Deep Seek gets to work. It scans the photos, identifies faces and objects, and cross-references them with the witness statements. It notices patterns you might have missed—a recurring license plate, a suspicious time gap, a subtle change in a suspect's behavior.

As you work together, Deep Seek doesn't just follow your instructions; it suggests new avenues of investigation. It's like having a partner who's always one step ahead, always thinking, always learning. By the end of the case, you've not only solved the mystery—you've gained a deeper understanding of how AI can enhance human intelligence.

This is just one example of what Deep Seek can do. As you read on, you'll discover countless other ways this remarkable model is transforming the world. So, let's dive in and explore the wonders of Deep Seek together. The quest for intelligence awaits!

CHAPTER 1:

The Birth of Deep Seek – A New Era in AI

Imagine standing on the edge of a vast, uncharted ocean. For centuries, humans have gazed at the horizon, wondering what lies beyond. Then, one day, someone invents a telescope—a tool that allows us to see farther than ever before. Suddenly, the unknown becomes knowable, and the impossible becomes possible.

This is the story of Deep Seek, the telescope of artificial intelligence. Just as the telescope revolutionized our understanding of the cosmos, Deep Seek is revolutionizing our understanding of intelligence itself. But to appreciate its significance, we must first journey back to its origins—to the moment when the seeds of Deep Seek were planted.

The Origins of Deep Seek: A Journey Through Time

The story of Deep Seek begins not in a lab or a tech company, but in the natural world. For billions of years, life on Earth has been driven by one fundamental force: the quest for survival.

From the tiniest microbes to the most complex organisms, every living thing has evolved to adapt, learn, and thrive in its environment.

At the heart of this process is the brain—nature's most sophisticated tool for processing information. The human brain, with its 86 billion neurons, is a marvel of evolution. It can recognize faces, solve problems, create art, and even ponder its own existence. For centuries, scientists have tried to understand how the brain works, and for decades, they've tried to replicate its abilities in machines.

This quest gave birth to the field of artificial intelligence (AI). Early AI systems were rudimentary, relying on simple rules and logic to perform tasks. But as technology advanced, so did our ambitions. In the 1980s, the rise of neural networks —computational models inspired by the brain—marked a turning point. These networks could learn from data, recognize patterns, and make decisions. However, they were limited by the technology of the time.

Fast forward to the 21st century, and we've entered the era of deep learning, where AI systems can process vast amounts of data, understand natural language, and even beat world champions at games like chess and Go. But even these systems have their limitations. They're powerful, but they're also passive —they wait for data to be fed to them, and they struggle to adapt to new situations.

This is where Deep Seek comes in. Unlike traditional AI models, Deep Seek doesn't just process information—it seeks it. It's proactive, curious, and adaptable, much like the human brain. But how did we get here? To answer that question, we need to explore the key milestones that led to the birth of Deep Seek.

The Inspiration: Learning from Nature

One of the most profound insights in AI research is that nature holds the key to solving some of our most complex problems. The human brain, with its ability to learn, adapt, and innovate, has been a constant source of inspiration for AI researchers. Deep Seek is no exception—it's deeply rooted in the principles of biological intelligence.

Neurons: The Building Blocks of Intelligence

At the core of both biological and artificial intelligence are neurons—tiny cells that process and transmit information. In the human brain, neurons are connected in vast networks, forming the basis of our thoughts, memories, and actions. In AI, artificial neurons are the building blocks of neural networks, the computational models that power systems like Deep Seek.

But while traditional neural networks are inspired by the brain, they're still a far cry from the real thing. The human brain is dynamic, constantly rewiring itself in response to new experiences. Deep Seek takes this idea a step further, creating a model that not only mimics the brain's structure but also its ability to adapt and evolve.

The Role of Curiosity

Another key inspiration for Deep Seek is the concept of curiosity. In humans, curiosity is what drives us to explore, learn, and innovate. It's what pushes us to ask questions, seek answers, and push the boundaries of what's possible. Deep Seek incorporates this idea into its design, creating a model that actively seeks out knowledge rather than passively waiting for it.

How Deep Seek Differs from Traditional AI Models

To understand why Deep Seek is such a big deal, it's important to understand how it differs from traditional AI models. Here are some key distinctions:

1. Proactive Learning

Traditional AI models are reactive—they wait for data to be fed to them before they can learn. Deep Seek, on the other hand, is proactive. It actively seeks out data, explores new possibilities, and learns from its environment. This makes it much more adaptable and versatile.

2. Contextual Understanding

Traditional AI models are good at recognizing patterns, but they often struggle to understand context. For example, a traditional model might recognize a cat in a photo, but it wouldn't understand the story behind the photo—why the cat is there, what it's doing, or how it's feeling. Deep Seek, with its ability to process and connect information, can grasp these nuances.

3. Human-Like Reasoning

One of the most exciting aspects of Deep Seek is its ability to reason like a human. Traditional AI models rely on brute force—processing vast amounts of data to find patterns. Deep Seek, on the other hand, uses a more intuitive approach, combining logic, creativity, and curiosity to solve problems.

The Analogy: Deep Seek as the Telescope of AI

To truly appreciate the significance of Deep Seek, let's return to our analogy of the telescope. For centuries, humans relied on their eyes to observe the world around them. But our eyes have limits—they can only see so far, and they can only perceive a small fraction of the electromagnetic spectrum.

Then, in the early 17th century, Galileo Galilei pointed a telescope at the night sky and changed everything. Suddenly, we could see distant stars, the craters of the moon, and the moons of Jupiter. The telescope didn't just extend our vision—it expanded our understanding of the universe.

Deep Seek is the telescope of AI. Just as the telescope allowed us to see beyond the limits of our eyes, Deep Seek allows us to think beyond the limits of traditional AI. It's a tool that extends our cognitive abilities, enabling us to explore new frontiers of knowledge and creativity.

A World Where Machines Can Think

Now, let's imagine a world where machines can think like humans. In this world, AI isn't just a tool—it's a partner. It's a colleague who helps us solve problems, a teacher who guides us through complex concepts, and a friend who understands our needs and desires.

In this world, Deep Seek is the key that unlocks this potential. It's the bridge between human and machine intelligence, combining the best of both worlds. With Deep Seek, we can tackle some of the most pressing challenges of our time—from curing diseases to combating climate change to exploring the cosmos.

The Road Ahead

The birth of Deep Seek marks the beginning of a new era in AI —an era where machines are not just tools, but collaborators. As we continue to explore the capabilities of Deep Seek, we'll uncover new possibilities, face new challenges, and push the boundaries of what's possible.

In the next chapter, we'll dive deeper into the building blocks of Deep Seek—the artificial neurons and networks that form the foundation of this revolutionary model. We'll explore how these components work together to create a system that's not just intelligent, but curious, adaptable, and endlessly fascinating.

So, are you ready to take the next step on this journey? Let's continue our quest for intelligence, one chapter at a time.

A Glimpse of What's to Come

To give you a taste of the journey ahead, here's a short scenario that illustrates the power of Deep Seek:

Scenario: The Curious Explorer

Imagine you're an explorer setting out to map an uncharted island. You have a traditional map, but it's incomplete—it only shows the coastline, not the interior. You also have a drone, but it's limited—it can only fly where you tell it to go.

Now, imagine you have Deep Seek. Instead of waiting for instructions, Deep Seek takes the initiative. It explores the island on its own, identifying landmarks, mapping terrain, and even predicting where you might find resources. It's like having a partner who's always one step ahead, always thinking, always learning.

By the end of your expedition, you've not only mapped the island—you've gained a deeper understanding of its ecosystem, its history, and its potential. And it's all thanks to Deep Seek.

This is just one example of what Deep Seek can do. As you read on, you'll discover countless other ways this remarkable model is transforming the world. So, let's dive in and explore the wonders of Deep Seek together. The quest for intelligence awaits!

CHAPTER 2:

The Building Blocks of Deep Seek – Neurons and Networks

Imagine you're at a bustling train station. People are rushing in every direction, conversations overlap, and announcements blare over the loudspeakers. Amidst this chaos, you spot a familiar face in the crowd—a friend you haven't seen in years. In an instant, your brain processes a flood of information: the shape of their face, the sound of their voice, the way they move. Without even thinking, you recognize them and call out their name.

This seemingly simple act is a marvel of human intelligence. It involves millions of neurons in your brain working together to process and interpret complex information. Now, imagine if a machine could do the same—recognize faces, understand voices, and make sense of the world around it. This is where Deep Seek comes in, and at its core are two fundamental components: artificial neurons and neural networks.

In this chapter, we'll explore these building blocks, how they work, and why they're so powerful. By the end, you'll understand how Deep Seek mimics the human brain to perform tasks that once seemed impossible for machines.

The Human Brain: Nature's Blueprint

To understand artificial neurons and neural networks, we first need to look at their inspiration: the human brain. The brain is made up of approximately 86 billion neurons, each connected to thousands of others. These neurons communicate through electrical and chemical signals, forming a vast network that processes information, makes decisions, and learns from experience.

A single neuron is like a tiny decision-maker. It receives inputs from other neurons, processes them, and decides whether to send an output signal. When billions of neurons work together, they create the complex behaviors we associate with intelligence —thinking, learning, and problem-solving.

Artificial Neurons: The Building Blocks of Deep Seek

Just as the human brain is built from neurons, Deep Seek is built from artificial neurons. These are simplified, mathematical versions of biological neurons designed to mimic their behavior. Let's break down how they work:

1. Inputs: Gathering Information

An artificial neuron receives inputs, which are numerical values representing data. For example, if the neuron is part of a system designed to recognize faces, the inputs might represent the pixels of an image.

2. Weights: Assigning Importance

Each input is multiplied by a weight, a number that determines its importance. For instance, in face recognition, certain features (like the eyes or nose) might be given higher weights because they're more critical for identification.

3. Summation: Combining Inputs

The weighted inputs are added together to produce a single value. This step is like gathering all the clues in a mystery and combining them to form a hypothesis.

4. Activation: Making a Decision

The summed value is passed through an activation function, which decides whether the neuron should "fire" (send an output signal). This is where the neuron makes its decision. For example, if the summed value exceeds a certain threshold, the neuron might conclude, "This looks like a face."

5. Output: Sending the Signal

If the neuron fires, it sends an output signal to other neurons in the network. This signal becomes an input for the next layer of neurons, continuing the process.

Neural Networks: A Team of Experts

While a single artificial neuron can make simple decisions, the real power lies in connecting many neurons together to form a neural network. Think of a neural network as a team of experts, each specializing in a specific task. By working together, they can solve complex problems that no single expert could handle alone.

Layers: Organizing the Team

A neural network is organized into layers:

Input Layer: This is where the network receives data, such as the pixels of an image.

Hidden Layers: These layers process the data, extracting features and patterns. Each hidden layer builds on the work of the previous one, refining the network's understanding.

Output Layer: This is where the network produces its final result, such as identifying a face or classifying an object.

Connections: Sharing Knowledge

The neurons in one layer are connected to neurons in the next layer through synapses, which are represented by weights. These connections allow information to flow through the network, with each layer contributing to the final decision.

The Analogy: Neurons as Team Members

To better understand how neural networks work, let's use an analogy. Imagine you're part of a team tasked with organizing a large event, like a music festival. Each team member has a specific role:

The Input Team: This group gathers information, such as the number of attendees, the lineup of artists, and the available venues.

The Hidden Teams: These teams process the information. One team might focus on logistics, another on marketing, and another on security. Each team builds on the work of the previous one, refining the plan.

The Output Team: This group consolidates all the information and makes the final decisions, such as setting the schedule and allocating resources.

Just like the neurons in a neural network, each team member contributes their expertise, and the connections between teams ensure that information flows smoothly. By working together, the team can organize a successful event—just as a neural network can solve complex problems.

A Real-Life Example: Recognizing Faces in a Crowd

Let's bring this to life with a real-world example: recognizing faces in a crowd. This is a task that Deep Seek excels at, and it's a great way to illustrate how neural networks function.

STEP 1: INPUT LAYER – RECEIVING THE IMAGE

The process begins when the network receives an image of a crowd. Each pixel in the image is converted into a numerical value, which becomes an input for the network.

STEP 2: HIDDEN LAYERS – EXTRACTING FEATURES

The hidden layers go to work, analyzing the image. The first hidden layer might detect simple features, like edges and lines. The next layer might combine these features to identify more complex patterns, like eyes, noses, and mouths. As the data moves through the layers, the network builds a detailed understanding of the image.

STEP 3: OUTPUT LAYER – MAKING THE DECISION

Finally, the output layer consolidates all the information and makes a decision. It might identify specific faces, classify them as "known" or "unknown," or even match them to a database of individuals.

The Role of Deep Seek

What sets Deep Seek apart is its ability to seek out the most relevant features. Instead of passively processing the image, it actively focuses on the most important details, like the shape of a face or the expression in the eyes. This makes it faster, more accurate, and more adaptable than traditional models.

Why This Matters: The Power of Neural Networks

Neural networks are the foundation of Deep Seek, and they're what make it so powerful. Here's why they matter:

Versatility: Neural networks can be applied to a wide range of tasks, from recognizing faces to translating languages to predicting weather patterns.

Adaptability: They can learn from data, improving their performance over time.

Scalability: By adding more layers and neurons, we can create networks capable of solving increasingly complex problems.

The Road Ahead

Now that we've explored the building blocks of Deep Seek, we're ready to dive deeper into how it works. In the next chapter, we'll explore the algorithmic heartbeat of Deep Seek—the processes that enable it to learn, adapt, and improve. We'll uncover the secrets of backpropagation and gradient descent, and we'll see how these algorithms power Deep Seek's incredible capabilities.

So, are you ready to continue the journey? Let's move forward and unlock the next layer of Deep Seek's mysteries.

A Glimpse of What's to Come

To give you a taste of what's ahead, here's a short scenario that illustrates the power of neural networks:

Scenario: The Language Translator

Imagine you're traveling in a foreign country, and you need to communicate with someone who doesn't speak your language. You pull out your phone and open a translation app powered by Deep Seek.

As you speak, the app converts your words into text, analyzes the meaning, and translates them into the other language. It's not just translating word for word—it's understanding the context, the tone, and the nuances of your speech.

By the end of the conversation, you've not only communicated effectively—you've experienced the power of neural networks in action.

This is just one example of what neural networks can do. As you read on, you'll discover countless other ways they're transforming the world. So, let's dive in and explore the wonders of Deep Seek together. The quest for intelligence awaits!

CHAPTER 3:

The Algorithmic Heartbeat – How Deep Seek Learns

Imagine you're teaching a child to ride a bike. At first, they wobble, fall, and struggle to balance. But with each attempt, they learn a little more—how to steer, how to pedal, how to stay upright. Over time, they get better, until one day, they're riding effortlessly, as if they've been doing it their whole life.

This process of learning through trial and error is at the heart of how Deep Seek works. Just like the child on the bike, Deep Seek learns by making mistakes, adjusting its approach, and improving over time. But instead of balancing on two wheels, Deep Seek is balancing equations, optimizing algorithms, and refining its understanding of the world.

In this chapter, we'll dive into the algorithmic heartbeat of Deep Seek—the core processes that enable it to learn, adapt, and improve. We'll explore backpropagation and gradient descent, two of the most important algorithms in AI, and we'll see how they power Deep Seek's incredible capabilities.

The Learning Process: A Journey of Trial and Error

At its core, learning is about making connections. Whether it's a child learning to ride a bike or a machine learning to recognize faces, the process involves trying, failing, and trying again. For Deep Seek, this process is guided by two key algorithms: backpropagation and gradient descent.

Backpropagation: Learning from Mistakes

Backpropagation is the process by which Deep Seek learns from its mistakes. Imagine you're playing darts. You throw a dart, and it lands far from the bullseye. You analyze your throw—maybe you aimed too high or used too much force—and adjust your technique for the next throw. Over time, your aim improves, and you hit the bullseye more often.

Backpropagation works in a similar way. When Deep Seek makes a prediction—say, identifying a face in an image—it compares its prediction to the correct answer. If it's wrong, it calculates how far off it was and adjusts the weights in its neural network to reduce the error. This process is repeated over and over, with each iteration bringing Deep Seek closer to the correct answer.

Gradient Descent: Finding the Optimal Path

Gradient descent is the algorithm that guides Deep Seek's adjustments. Imagine you're hiking in the mountains, trying to find the lowest point in a valley. You can't see the entire landscape, so you take small steps, always moving downhill. Eventually, you reach the bottom.

Gradient descent works in a similar way. It calculates the gradient—a measure of how much the error changes with respect to the weights—and adjusts the weights in the direction that reduces the error. This process is like taking small steps downhill, gradually finding the optimal set of weights that minimize the error.

The Analogy: Deep Seek as a Student

To better understand how Deep Seek learns, let's use an analogy. Imagine Deep Seek is a student preparing for a math exam. The student starts by solving practice problems, but they make mistakes along the way. Here's how the learning process unfolds:

Initial Attempt: The student solves a problem but gets the wrong answer.

Error Calculation: The student compares their answer to the correct one and calculates how far off they were.

Adjustment: The student reviews their steps, identifies where they went wrong, and adjusts their approach.

Repeat: The student solves the problem again, this time with a better understanding.

Over time, the student's performance improves, and they're able to solve problems more accurately and efficiently. This is exactly how Deep Seek learns—by making mistakes, analyzing them, and refining its approach.

A Scenario: Deep Seek Learns to Play a Game

Let's bring this to life with a scenario: Deep Seek learning to play a game. For this example, we'll use Tic-Tac-Toe, a simple but strategic game that's perfect for illustrating the learning process.

STEP 1: INITIAL MOVES

At first, Deep Seek plays randomly, making moves without any strategy. It might place its X in a corner, the center, or even a losing position. Unsurprisingly, it loses most of its games.

STEP 2: ERROR CALCULATION

After each game, Deep Seek analyzes the outcome. If it loses, it calculates the error—the difference between its moves and the optimal strategy. It identifies which moves led to the loss and assigns a higher error to those decisions.

STEP 3: BACKPROPAGATION

Using backpropagation, Deep Seek adjusts the weights in its neural network to reduce the error. It "learns" that certain moves (like taking the center) are more likely to lead to a win, while others (like leaving a winning move open for the opponent) are more likely to lead to a loss.

STEP 4: GRADIENT DESCENT

Gradient descent guides the adjustments, ensuring that Deep Seek takes small, calculated steps toward the optimal strategy. It doesn't overhaul its entire approach at once—it makes incremental improvements, gradually refining its understanding of the game.

STEP 5: MASTERY

After thousands of games, Deep Seek becomes a master of Tic-Tac-Toe. It no longer makes random moves—it anticipates the opponent's strategy, blocks winning moves, and sets up its own victories. It's learned through trial and error, just like a human player.

Why This Matters: The Power of Learning Algorithms

Backpropagation and gradient descent are the engines that power Deep Seek's learning process. Here's why they're so important:

Adaptability: These algorithms allow Deep Seek to adapt to new tasks and environments, making it versatile and powerful.

Efficiency: By learning from mistakes and optimizing its approach, Deep Seek can achieve high levels of accuracy with relatively little data.

Scalability: These algorithms can be applied to a wide range of problems, from playing games to diagnosing diseases to predicting stock prices.

The Road Ahead

Now that we've explored the algorithmic heartbeat of Deep Seek, we're ready to dive deeper into its inner workings. In the next chapter, we'll explore the power of data—the fuel that drives Deep Seek's learning process. We'll see how data is collected, processed, and used to train Deep Seek, and we'll uncover the secrets of data augmentation and feature extraction.

So, are you ready to continue the journey? Let's move forward and unlock the next layer of Deep Seek's mysteries.

A Glimpse of What's to Come

To give you a taste of what's ahead, here's a short scenario that illustrates the power of learning algorithms:

Scenario: The Language Learner

Imagine Deep Seek is learning to translate languages. At first, its translations are clumsy and inaccurate. But with each mistake, it adjusts its approach, refining its understanding of grammar, vocabulary, and context. Over time, its translations become fluent and natural, capturing the nuances of human language.

By the end of the process, Deep Seek is not just translating words —it's conveying meaning, tone, and emotion. It's a testament to the power of learning algorithms and their ability to transform raw data into intelligence.

This is just one example of what Deep Seek can do. As you read on, you'll discover countless other ways it's transforming the world. So, let's dive in and explore the wonders of Deep Seek together. The quest for intelligence awaits!

CHAPTER 4:

The Power of Data – Fueling Deep Seek's Intelligence

Imagine you're training for a marathon. To perform at your best, you need the right fuel—nutritious food that gives you energy, builds your strength, and helps you recover. Without it, no matter how hard you train, you'll never reach your full potential.

In the world of artificial intelligence, data is the fuel that powers models like Deep Seek. Just as food fuels the human body, data fuels the learning process, enabling Deep Seek to recognize patterns, make decisions, and improve over time. But not all data is created equal. Just as junk food can hinder your performance, poor-quality data can limit Deep Seek's capabilities.

In this chapter, we'll explore the role of data in training Deep Seek. We'll discuss how data is collected, preprocessed, and augmented, and we'll see how it drives Deep Seek's intelligence. Along the way, we'll use the example of a self-driving car to illustrate how data fuels one of the most exciting applications of AI.

The Role of Data: The Fuel for Intelligence

Data is the foundation of Deep Seek's learning process. Without data, Deep Seek would be like a car without fuel—powerless and unable to move. But what exactly is data, and why is it so important?

What is Data?

In the context of AI, data refers to any information that can be used to train a model. This could be images, text, audio, sensor readings, or any other type of input. For example, a self-driving car might use data from cameras, radar, and GPS to navigate its environment.

Why is Data Important?

Data is what enables Deep Seek to learn. By analyzing vast amounts of data, Deep Seek can identify patterns, make predictions, and improve its performance. The more data Deep Seek has, the better it can learn—but only if the data is high-quality and relevant.

The Data Pipeline: From Collection to Training

The process of using data to train Deep Seek involves several steps, each of which is critical to the model's success. Let's break down the data pipeline:

1. Data Collection: Gathering the Raw Materials

The first step is to collect data. This could involve taking photos, recording audio, or gathering sensor readings. For example, a self-driving car might collect data by driving through different environments, capturing images of roads, traffic signs, and pedestrians.

2. Data Preprocessing: Cleaning and Organizing

Raw data is often messy and unstructured. Before it can be used to train Deep Seek, it needs to be cleaned and organized. This might involve:

Removing noise: Filtering out irrelevant or corrupted data.

Normalizing: Scaling data to a standard range, such as converting pixel values to a range of 0 to 1.

Labeling: Adding tags or annotations to the data, such as identifying objects in an image.

3. Data Augmentation: Expanding the Dataset

Data augmentation is the process of creating new data from existing data. This is especially useful when the dataset is small or lacks diversity. For example, a self-driving car's dataset might be augmented by flipping images horizontally, adjusting brightness, or adding simulated weather conditions like rain or fog.

4. Training: Feeding Data to Deep Seek

Once the data is collected, preprocessed, and augmented, it's fed into Deep Seek for training. During training, Deep Seek analyzes the data, learns from it, and adjusts its internal parameters to improve its performance.

The Analogy: Data as Fuel for the Brain

To better understand the role of data, let's use an analogy. Imagine the human brain is a high-performance car, and data is the fuel that powers it. Just as a car needs the right type and amount of fuel to run efficiently, the brain needs high-quality data to function at its best.

Quality Matters: Just as low-quality fuel can damage a car's engine, low-quality data can hinder Deep Seek's performance. For example, if a self-driving car's dataset contains blurry or mislabeled images, it might struggle to recognize obstacles or navigate safely.

Quantity Matters: A car needs enough fuel to reach its destination, and Deep Seek needs enough data to learn effectively. A small dataset might not provide enough information for Deep Seek to generalize to new situations.

Diversity Matters: Just as a car needs a balanced mix of fuel types, Deep Seek needs diverse data to handle a wide range of scenarios. For example, a self-driving car's dataset should include data from different weather conditions, times of day, and road types.

A Scenario: A Self-Driving Car Learns to Navigate

Let's bring this to life with a scenario: a self-driving car learning to navigate through different environments. This is one of the most complex and exciting applications of AI, and it relies heavily on data.

STEP 1: DATA COLLECTION

The self-driving car is equipped with cameras, radar, and other sensors. As it drives, it collects data about its surroundings—images of the road, readings from its radar, and GPS coordinates. This data is stored and used to train Deep Seek.

STEP 2: DATA PREPROCESSING

The raw data is cleaned and organized. For example:

Blurry or corrupted images are removed.

Radar readings are normalized to a standard range.

Objects in the images are labeled, such as identifying pedestrians, vehicles, and traffic signs.

STEP 3: DATA AUGMENTATION

To expand the dataset, the data is augmented. For example:

Images are flipped horizontally to simulate driving in the opposite direction.

Brightness and contrast are adjusted to simulate different lighting conditions.

Simulated rain or fog is added to images to prepare the car for adverse weather.

STEP 4: TRAINING DEEP SEEK

The preprocessed and augmented data is fed into Deep Seek for training. Deep Seek analyzes the data, learning to recognize patterns and make decisions. For example:

It learns to identify pedestrians and predict their movements.

It learns to recognize traffic signs and obey traffic rules.

It learns to navigate complex intersections and avoid obstacles.

STEP 5: TESTING AND REFINEMENT

Once trained, the self-driving car is tested in real-world conditions. Any mistakes it makes are analyzed, and the data is used to further refine Deep Seek's performance. Over time, the car becomes more accurate, reliable, and safe.

Why This Matters: The Power of Data

Data is the lifeblood of Deep Seek, and its importance cannot be overstated. Here's why data matters:

Accuracy: High-quality data enables Deep Seek to make accurate predictions and decisions.

Adaptability: Diverse data allows Deep Seek to handle a wide range of scenarios and environments.

Innovation: New types of data, such as sensor data from self-driving cars, enable new applications of AI.

The Road Ahead

Now that we've explored the power of data, we're ready to dive deeper into the training process. In the next chapter, we'll explore the art of training—how Deep Seek learns from data, adjusts its parameters, and improves over time. We'll uncover the secrets of epochs, batches, and loss functions, and we'll see how these concepts drive Deep Seek's learning process.

So, are you ready to continue the journey? Let's move forward and unlock the next layer of Deep Seek's mysteries.

A Glimpse of What's to Come

To give you a taste of what's ahead, here's a short scenario that illustrates the power of training:

Scenario: The Language Translator

Imagine Deep Seek is learning to translate languages. At first, its translations are clumsy and inaccurate. But with each iteration of training, it adjusts its parameters, refining its understanding of grammar, vocabulary, and context. Over time, its translations become fluent and natural, capturing the nuances of human language.

By the end of the process, Deep Seek is not just translating words —it's conveying meaning, tone, and emotion. It's a testament to the power of data and the training process.

This is just one example of what Deep Seek can do. As you read on, you'll discover countless other ways it's transforming the world. So, let's dive in and explore the wonders of Deep Seek together. The quest for intelligence awaits!

CHAPTER 5:

The Art of Training – Teaching Deep Seek to Think

Imagine you're teaching a child to ride a bike. At first, they wobble, fall, and struggle to balance. But with each attempt, they learn a little more—how to steer, how to pedal, how to stay upright. Over time, they get better, until one day, they're riding effortlessly, as if they've been doing it their whole life.

This process of learning through trial and error is at the heart of how Deep Seek is trained. Just like the child on the bike, Deep Seek learns by making mistakes, adjusting its approach, and improving over time. But instead of balancing on two wheels, Deep Seek is balancing equations, optimizing algorithms, and refining its understanding of the world.

In this chapter, we'll explore the art of training—the process by which Deep Seek learns from data, adjusts its parameters, and improves its performance. We'll dive into key concepts like epochs, batches, and loss functions, and we'll see how they work together to teach Deep Seek to think.

The Training Process: A Journey of Iteration

Training Deep Seek is an iterative process. It involves repeatedly exposing the model to data, evaluating its performance, and making adjustments to improve its accuracy. Let's break down the key components of this process:

1. Epochs: Learning Through Repetition

An epoch is one complete pass through the entire training dataset. Think of it as a practice session for Deep Seek. During each epoch, Deep Seek analyzes the data, makes predictions, and adjusts its parameters to reduce errors.

For example, if Deep Seek is learning to recognize flowers, each epoch involves showing it images of different flowers and teaching it to identify them correctly. The more epochs Deep Seek goes through, the better it becomes at recognizing flowers.

2. Batches: Breaking Down the Data

Training on the entire dataset at once can be computationally expensive. To make the process more efficient, the data is divided into smaller groups called batches. Each batch is processed separately, and Deep Seek updates its parameters after each batch.

Using the flower example, instead of showing Deep Seek all the flower images at once, we might divide them into batches of 32 images each. Deep Seek processes one batch at a time, learning from each group of images before moving on to the next.

3. Loss Functions: Measuring Mistakes

A loss function is a mathematical formula that measures how far off Deep Seek's predictions are from the correct answers. It quantifies the error, providing a clear target for Deep Seek to minimize.

For example, if Deep Seek misidentifies a rose as a tulip, the loss function calculates how wrong the prediction was. Deep Seek then adjusts its parameters to reduce this error in future predictions.

The Analogy: Teaching a Child to Ride a Bike

To better understand the training process, let's use the analogy of teaching a child to ride a bike. Here's how it maps to Deep Seek's training:

Epochs as Practice Sessions: Each time the child gets on the bike and tries to ride, it's like an epoch. With each attempt, they learn a little more and get a little better.

Batches as Small Steps: Instead of trying to ride the bike perfectly on the first attempt, the child takes small steps— balancing, pedaling, steering. Each step is like a batch, helping them build confidence and skill.

Loss Functions as Feedback: When the child falls, they get feedback—what went wrong, how to adjust. This feedback is like the loss function, guiding them toward better performance.

Over time, the child becomes a skilled bike rider, just as Deep Seek becomes a skilled model through training.

A Scenario: Deep Seek Learns to Recognize Flowers

Let's bring this to life with a scenario: Deep Seek learning to recognize different species of flowers. This is a classic example of a classification task, where the goal is to assign each input (an image of a flower) to a specific category (the type of flower).

STEP 1: PREPARING THE DATA

The first step is to gather and preprocess the data. This might involve:

Collecting images of different flowers, such as roses, tulips, and daisies.

Labeling each image with the correct species.

Dividing the data into training and testing sets.

STEP 2: TRAINING DEEP SEEK

Now, the training process begins. Here's how it unfolds:

First Epoch: Deep Seek is shown the first batch of flower images. It makes predictions, but they're mostly wrong. The loss function calculates the errors, and Deep Seek adjusts its parameters to reduce them.

Subsequent Epochs: With each epoch, Deep Seek gets better at recognizing flowers. It learns to distinguish between a rose's petals and a tulip's shape, refining its understanding with each batch.

Final Epoch: By the last epoch, Deep Seek's predictions are highly accurate. It can confidently identify roses, tulips, daisies, and more.

STEP 3: TESTING AND REFINEMENT

Once training is complete, Deep Seek is tested on a separate set of flower images it has never seen before. This ensures that it can generalize its learning to new data. Any mistakes are analyzed, and the training process is refined to further improve performance.

Why This Matters: The Power of Training

The training process is what transforms Deep Seek from a blank slate into a powerful AI model. Here's why it matters:

Accuracy: Through training, Deep Seek learns to make accurate predictions and decisions.

Adaptability: Training allows Deep Seek to adapt to new tasks and environments, making it versatile and robust.

Innovation: Advances in training techniques, such as transfer learning and reinforcement learning, enable new applications of AI.

The Road Ahead

Now that we've explored the art of training, we're ready to dive deeper into the inner workings of Deep Seek. In the next chapter, we'll explore the magic of layers—how Deep Seek's neural networks are organized into layers, and how each layer contributes to the model's understanding of the world.

So, are you ready to continue the journey? Let's move forward and unlock the next layer of Deep Seek's mysteries.

A Glimpse of What's to Come

To give you a taste of what's ahead, here's a short scenario that illustrates the power of layers:

Scenario: The Image Analyzer

Imagine Deep Seek is analyzing a complex image, such as a cityscape. The first layer detects simple features, like edges and lines. The next layer combines these features to identify shapes, like windows and doors. The final layer recognizes objects, like buildings and cars.

By the end of the process, Deep Seek has not only identified the objects in the image—it's understood the scene as a whole. It's a testament to the power of layers and their role in Deep Seek's intelligence.

This is just one example of what Deep Seek can do. As you read on, you'll discover countless other ways it's transforming the world. So, let's dive in and explore the wonders of Deep Seek together. The quest for intelligence awaits!

CHAPTER 6:

The Magic of Layers – Deep Learning in Action

Imagine peeling an onion. As you remove each layer, you uncover something new—a different texture, a stronger scent, a deeper color. Each layer adds to your understanding of the onion as a whole, revealing its complexity and richness.

This is how Deep Seek works. At its core, Deep Seek is a deep learning model, which means it's composed of multiple layers of artificial neurons. Each layer processes information in a different way, extracting increasingly complex features and building a deeper understanding of the data. Just like the layers of an onion, each layer in Deep Seek reveals a new level of insight, transforming raw data into meaningful intelligence.

In this chapter, we'll explore the magic of layers—how they work, why they're important, and how they enable Deep Seek to perform tasks that once seemed impossible for machines. Along the way, we'll use the example of Deep Seek analyzing a cityscape to illustrate the power of layers in action.

What is Deep Learning?

Deep learning is a subset of machine learning that uses neural networks with multiple layers to model complex patterns in data. The term "deep" refers to the number of layers in the network—the more layers, the "deeper" the model.

Deep learning has revolutionized AI, enabling breakthroughs in areas like image recognition, natural language processing, and autonomous driving. But what makes deep learning so powerful? The answer lies in the layers.

The Role of Layers: Building Understanding Step by Step

Each layer in a deep learning model has a specific role to play. Let's break down how layers work and why they're so important:

1. Input Layer: Receiving the Data

The input layer is where the model receives its data. For example, if Deep Seek is analyzing an image of a cityscape, the input layer would receive the pixel values of the image.

2. Hidden Layers: Extracting Features

The hidden layers are where the magic happens. Each hidden layer processes the data in a different way, extracting increasingly complex features:

First Hidden Layer: Detects simple features, like edges and lines.

Second Hidden Layer: Combines these features to identify shapes, like windows and doors.

Third Hidden Layer: Recognizes objects, like buildings and cars.

3. Output Layer: Making the Decision

The output layer consolidates all the information and produces the final result. For example, if Deep Seek is classifying the cityscape, the output layer might identify specific objects or generate a description of the scene.

The Analogy: Layers of an Onion

To better understand the role of layers, let's use the analogy of an onion. Imagine the data is the onion, and each layer in Deep Seek is a layer of the onion:

Outer Layer (Input Layer): The outer layer of the onion is like the input layer of Deep Seek. It's the first point of contact with the data, receiving the raw input.

Middle Layers (Hidden Layers): As you peel away the outer layers, you uncover deeper, more complex layers. These are like the hidden layers of Deep Seek, each revealing new features and insights.

Core (Output Layer): At the center of the onion is the core, where all the layers come together. This is like the output layer of Deep Seek, where the final decision is made.

Just as peeling an onion reveals its complexity, processing data through multiple layers reveals the richness and depth of the information.

A Scenario: Deep Seek Analyzes a Cityscape

Let's bring this to life with a scenario: Deep Seek analyzing a complex image of a cityscape. This is a classic example of a computer vision task, where the goal is to understand and interpret visual data.

STEP 1: INPUT LAYER – RECEIVING THE IMAGE

The process begins when Deep Seek receives an image of a cityscape. The input layer processes the pixel values, converting the image into a format that the model can work with.

STEP 2: FIRST HIDDEN LAYER – DETECTING EDGES

The first hidden layer analyzes the image and detects simple features, like edges and lines. For example, it might identify the outlines of buildings, the curves of roads, and the shapes of windows.

STEP 3: SECOND HIDDEN LAYER – IDENTIFYING SHAPES

The second hidden layer builds on the work of the first layer, combining edges and lines to identify more complex shapes. For example, it might recognize the rectangular shape of a building, the circular shape of a traffic light, and the triangular shape of a roof.

STEP 4: THIRD HIDDEN LAYER – RECOGNIZING OBJECTS

The third hidden layer takes things a step further, recognizing entire objects. For example, it might identify a car, a pedestrian, and a street sign. At this point, Deep Seek is starting to understand the scene as a whole.

STEP 5: OUTPUT LAYER – GENERATING A DESCRIPTION

Finally, the output layer consolidates all the information and produces a description of the cityscape. For example, it might generate a sentence like, "A busy city street with tall buildings, cars, and pedestrians."

Why This Matters: The Power of Layers

Layers are what make deep learning so powerful. Here's why they matter:

Hierarchical Understanding: Layers enable Deep Seek to build a hierarchical understanding of data, from simple features to complex concepts.

Feature Extraction: Each layer extracts different features, allowing Deep Seek to capture the richness and diversity of the data.

Scalability: By adding more layers, we can create models capable of solving increasingly complex problems.

The Road Ahead

Now that we've explored the magic of layers, we're ready to dive deeper into the inner workings of Deep Seek. In the next chapter, we'll explore the vision of Deep Seek—how it processes visual information, from images to videos, and how it's transforming the field of computer vision.

So, are you ready to continue the journey? Let's move forward and unlock the next layer of Deep Seek's mysteries.

A Glimpse of What's to Come

To give you a taste of what's ahead, here's a short scenario that illustrates the power of computer vision:

Scenario: The Medical Diagnostician

Imagine Deep Seek is analyzing medical images, such as X-rays or MRIs. The first layer detects simple features, like edges and shapes. The next layer identifies more complex patterns, like tumors or fractures. The final layer generates a diagnosis, helping doctors make informed decisions.

By the end of the process, Deep Seek has not only analyzed the images—it's provided valuable insights that can save lives. It's a testament to the power of layers and their role in Deep Seek's intelligence.

This is just one example of what Deep Seek can do. As you read on, you'll discover countless other ways it's transforming the world. So, let's dive in and explore the wonders of Deep Seek together. The quest for intelligence awaits!

CHAPTER 7:

The Vision of Deep Seek – Seeing the World Through AI Eyes

Imagine you're looking at a photograph of a park. In an instant, your brain processes the scene—the lush green grass, the towering trees, the playful dog chasing a frisbee, and the serene lake in the background. You don't just see shapes and colors; you understand the story the image tells. Now, imagine if a machine could do the same—not just capture pixels, but truly see and interpret the world.

This is the power of Deep Seek's vision. At the heart of this capability are convolutional neural networks (CNNs), a specialized type of neural network designed to process visual information. CNNs enable Deep Seek to analyze images, recognize objects, and even understand context, much like the human visual system.

In this chapter, we'll explore how Deep Seek processes visual information, the role of CNNs, and how this technology is transforming fields like healthcare, autonomous driving, and more. Along the way, we'll use the example of Deep Seek identifying objects in a photo—such as distinguishing between a cat and a dog—to illustrate the magic of AI vision.

How Deep Seek Processes Visual Information

When Deep Seek "sees" an image, it doesn't perceive it the way humans do. Instead, it processes the image as a grid of numerical values, where each number represents the color and intensity of a pixel. The challenge is to transform this grid of numbers into meaningful information—like recognizing a cat or a dog. This is where convolutional neural networks (CNNs) come in.

What Are Convolutional Neural Networks (CNNs)?

CNNs are a type of neural network specifically designed for processing visual data. They are inspired by the human visual system, where different parts of the brain are responsible for recognizing different aspects of an image, such as edges, shapes, and objects.

Key Components of CNNs

Convolutional Layers: These layers apply filters to the image to detect features like edges, textures, and patterns. Each filter focuses on a specific aspect of the image, such as horizontal lines or diagonal edges.

Pooling Layers: These layers reduce the size of the image while preserving the most important information. This makes the model more efficient and helps it focus on the most relevant features.

Fully Connected Layers: These layers combine the features detected by the convolutional layers to make final decisions, such as classifying an object.

The Analogy: CNNs and the Human Visual System

To better understand how CNNs work, let's compare them to the human visual system. Imagine your brain as a team of experts, each specializing in a different aspect of vision:

Edge Detectors: Some experts are responsible for detecting edges and lines in the image. They identify the boundaries of objects, like the outline of a cat or a dog.

Shape Recognizers: Other experts focus on combining edges to recognize shapes, like the round face of a cat or the elongated snout of a dog.

Object Identifiers: Finally, a group of experts combines all the information to identify the object as a whole—recognizing it as a cat or a dog.

This is exactly how CNNs work. Each layer in the network specializes in a different task, building a hierarchical understanding of the image.

A Scenario: Deep Seek Identifies a Cat and a Dog

Let's bring this to life with a scenario: Deep Seek analyzing a photo of a cat and a dog. Here's how the process unfolds:

STEP 1: INPUT LAYER – RECEIVING THE IMAGE

The process begins when Deep Seek receives the photo. The input layer processes the pixel values, converting the image into a grid of numbers.

STEP 2: CONVOLUTIONAL LAYERS – DETECTING FEATURES

The convolutional layers analyze the image, applying filters to detect features:

The first convolutional layer detects simple features, like edges and textures. For example, it might identify the outline of the cat's ears or the dog's tail.

The second convolutional layer combines these features to recognize more complex patterns, like the shape of the cat's face or the dog's snout.

STEP 3: POOLING LAYERS – SIMPLIFYING THE IMAGE

The pooling layers reduce the size of the image while preserving the most important features. This helps Deep Seek focus on the key aspects of the image, like the cat's eyes or the dog's fur.

STEP 4: FULLY CONNECTED LAYERS – MAKING THE DECISION

The fully connected layers combine all the features detected by the convolutional layers to make a final decision. For example:

They might recognize the cat's triangular ears and whiskers, classifying it as a cat.

They might identify the dog's floppy ears and wagging tail, classifying it as a dog.

STEP 5: OUTPUT LAYER – GENERATING THE RESULT

Finally, the output layer produces the result. Deep Seek might generate a label like "cat" or "dog," or even provide a confidence score, such as "90% cat, 10% dog."

Why This Matters: The Power of AI Vision

Deep Seek's ability to process visual information has transformative implications. Here's why it matters:

Accuracy: CNNs enable Deep Seek to recognize objects with remarkable accuracy, even in complex or cluttered scenes.

Speed: Deep Seek can process images in real-time, making it ideal for applications like autonomous driving and surveillance.

Versatility: CNNs can be applied to a wide range of tasks, from medical imaging to facial recognition to art generation.

Real-World Applications of Deep Seek's Vision

Deep Seek's vision capabilities are already being used in a variety of fields:

1. Healthcare

Deep Seek can analyze medical images, such as X-rays and MRIs, to detect diseases like cancer or fractures. For example, it might identify a tumor in a lung X-ray or a fracture in a bone scan.

2. Autonomous Driving

Deep Seek enables self-driving cars to "see" the road, recognize obstacles, and make decisions in real-time. For example, it might identify a pedestrian crossing the street or a stop sign at an intersection.

3. Retail

Deep Seek can analyze customer behavior in stores, tracking movements and identifying trends. For example, it might recognize which products customers are most interested in or how they navigate the store.

The Road Ahead

Now that we've explored Deep Seek's vision capabilities, we're ready to dive deeper into its ability to understand language. In the next chapter, we'll explore the language of machines —how Deep Seek processes and generates text, and how it's transforming fields like translation, content creation, and customer service.

So, are you ready to continue the journey? Let's move forward and unlock the next layer of Deep Seek's mysteries.

A Glimpse of What's to Come

To give you a taste of what's ahead, here's a short scenario that illustrates the power of language processing:

Scenario: The Language Translator

Imagine Deep Seek is translating a sentence from English to French. It doesn't just translate word for word—it understands the context, the tone, and the nuances of the language. By the end of the process, the translation is fluent and natural, capturing the essence of the original sentence.

This is the power of Deep Seek's language capabilities, and it's just the beginning of what's possible.

This is just one example of what Deep Seek can do. As you read on, you'll discover countless other ways it's transforming the world. So, let's dive in and explore the wonders of Deep Seek together. The quest for intelligence awaits!

CHAPTER 8:

The Language of Machines – Deep Seek's Understanding of Text

Imagine you're learning a new language. At first, the words sound like gibberish, the grammar feels like a puzzle, and the nuances of meaning seem impossible to grasp. But over time, you start to recognize patterns—the way verbs conjugate, the way sentences are structured, the way context shapes meaning. Eventually, you're not just translating words; you're understanding ideas, emotions, and stories.

This is the journey of Deep Seek as it learns to process and understand text. At the heart of this capability is natural language processing (NLP), a branch of AI that focuses on enabling machines to understand, interpret, and generate human language. NLP allows Deep Seek to perform tasks like translation, sentiment analysis, and content creation, transforming the way we interact with machines.

In this chapter, we'll explore how Deep Seek processes and understands text, the role of NLP techniques, and how this technology is bridging the gap between humans and machines. Along the way, we'll use the example of Deep Seek translating a sentence from one language to another to illustrate the magic of

AI language understanding.

How Deep Seek Processes Text

When Deep Seek "reads" text, it doesn't perceive it the way humans do. Instead, it processes the text as a sequence of numerical values, where each word or character is represented by a number. The challenge is to transform this sequence of numbers into meaningful information—like understanding the meaning of a sentence or generating a response. This is where natural language processing (NLP) comes in.

What is Natural Language Processing (NLP)?

NLP is a field of AI that focuses on enabling machines to understand, interpret, and generate human language. It involves a combination of linguistics, computer science, and machine learning techniques. Here are some key components of NLP:

Tokenization: Breaking text into smaller units, such as words or characters.

Embeddings: Representing words or phrases as numerical vectors, capturing their meaning and relationships.

Syntax Analysis: Understanding the grammatical structure of sentences.

Semantic Analysis: Interpreting the meaning of words and sentences in context.

Contextual Understanding: Capturing the broader context of a conversation or document.

The Analogy: Learning a New Language

To better understand how NLP works, let's compare it to learning a new language. Imagine Deep Seek is a student trying to learn French:

Tokenization (Learning Words): The first step is to learn individual words. Deep Seek breaks down French sentences into words, just like a student might memorize vocabulary.

Embeddings (Understanding Meaning): Next, Deep Seek learns the meaning of each word and how it relates to others. For example, it might learn that "chat" means "cat" and is related to "animal."

Syntax Analysis (Learning Grammar): Deep Seek then learns the rules of grammar, such as how verbs conjugate and how sentences are structured.

Semantic Analysis (Understanding Context): Finally, Deep Seek learns to interpret the meaning of sentences in context. For example, it might understand that "Il fait beau" means "The weather is nice" and is often used in casual conversation.

By combining these steps, Deep Seek becomes fluent in French, just like a human learner.

A Scenario: Deep Seek Translates a Sentence

Let's bring this to life with a scenario: Deep Seek translating a sentence from English to French. Here's how the process unfolds:

STEP 1: TOKENIZATION – BREAKING DOWN THE SENTENCE

The process begins when Deep Seek receives the English sentence: "The cat is sitting on the mat." It breaks the sentence into individual words: ["The", "cat", "is", "sitting", "on", "the", "mat"].

STEP 2: EMBEDDINGS – UNDERSTANDING MEANING

Deep Seek converts each word into a numerical vector, capturing its meaning and relationships. For example:

"Cat" might be represented as a vector close to "animal" and "pet."

"Sitting" might be represented as a vector close to "resting" and "position."

STEP 3: SYNTAX ANALYSIS – UNDERSTANDING GRAMMAR

Deep Seek analyzes the grammatical structure of the sentence. It recognizes that:

"The cat" is the subject.

"Is sitting" is the verb phrase.

"On the mat" is the prepositional phrase.

STEP 4: SEMANTIC ANALYSIS – UNDERSTANDING CONTEXT

Deep Seek interprets the meaning of the sentence in context. It understands that the sentence describes a cat resting on a mat, a common and relatable scenario.

STEP 5: TRANSLATION – GENERATING THE FRENCH SENTENCE

Finally, Deep Seek generates the French translation: "Le chat est assis sur le tapis." It doesn't just translate word for word—it captures the nuances of meaning, ensuring the translation is fluent and natural.

Why This Matters: The Power of NLP

Deep Seek's ability to process and understand text has transformative implications. Here's why it matters:

Communication: NLP enables Deep Seek to bridge language barriers, making it easier for people to communicate across cultures.

Automation: NLP automates tasks like customer service, content creation, and data analysis, saving time and resources.

Insights: NLP allows Deep Seek to analyze large volumes of text, uncovering patterns and insights that would be impossible for humans to detect.

Real-World Applications of Deep Seek's NLP Capabilities

Deep Seek's NLP capabilities are already being used in a variety of fields:

1. Translation

Deep Seek powers translation tools like Google Translate, enabling real-time communication across languages.

2. Sentiment Analysis

Deep Seek analyzes social media posts, reviews, and surveys to gauge public opinion and sentiment.

3. Chatbots

Deep Seek enables chatbots to understand and respond to customer queries, providing personalized and efficient support.

4. Content Creation

Deep Seek generates articles, summaries, and even poetry, assisting writers and content creators.

The Road Ahead

Now that we've explored Deep Seek's language capabilities,

we're ready to dive deeper into its ability to process audio. In the next chapter, we'll explore the sound of intelligence—how Deep Seek processes and understands audio data, from speech to music, and how it's transforming fields like voice assistants, transcription, and sound analysis.

So, are you ready to continue the journey? Let's move forward and unlock the next layer of Deep Seek's mysteries.

A Glimpse of What's to Come

To give you a taste of what's ahead, here's a short scenario that illustrates the power of audio processing:

Scenario: The Voice Assistant

Imagine Deep Seek is powering a voice assistant like Siri or Alexa. You ask it to play your favorite song, and it understands your request, even if you mumble or speak quickly. It not only plays the song but also adjusts the volume based on your tone of voice.

This is the power of Deep Seek's audio capabilities, and it's just the beginning of what's possible.

This is just one example of what Deep Seek can do. As you read on, you'll discover countless other ways it's transforming the world. So, let's dive in and explore the wonders of Deep Seek together. The quest for intelligence awaits!

CHAPTER 9:

The Sound of Intelligence – Deep Seek's Auditory Skills

Imagine you're at a crowded café. The clatter of dishes, the hum of conversations, and the faint melody of background music fill the air. Amidst this noise, you hear a friend call your name. Instantly, your brain filters out the irrelevant sounds, focuses on the voice, and processes the words. This ability to hear, interpret, and understand sound is a marvel of human intelligence.

Now, imagine if a machine could do the same—not just record sound, but truly listen and understand it. This is the power of Deep Seek's auditory skills. At the heart of this capability are advanced techniques for processing audio data, including speech recognition and sound analysis. These skills enable Deep Seek to transcribe conversations, identify sounds, and even generate music, transforming the way we interact with machines.

In this chapter, we'll explore how Deep Seek processes audio data, the role of speech recognition and sound analysis, and how this technology is revolutionizing fields like voice assistants, transcription, and sound design. Along the way, we'll use the example of Deep Seek transcribing a spoken conversation to illustrate the magic of AI auditory skills.

How Deep Seek Processes Audio Data

When Deep Seek "hears" sound, it doesn't perceive it the way humans do. Instead, it processes the sound as a sequence of numerical values, where each number represents the amplitude and frequency of the sound wave. The challenge is to transform this sequence of numbers into meaningful information—like recognizing speech or identifying a melody. This is where audio processing techniques come in.

Key Components of Audio Processing

Deep Seek's ability to process audio data relies on several key techniques:

1. Speech Recognition

Speech recognition is the process of converting spoken language into text. It involves:

Acoustic Modeling: Analyzing the sound waves to identify phonemes (the smallest units of sound).

Language Modeling: Understanding the structure and meaning of sentences.

Decoding: Combining acoustic and language models to generate the most likely transcription.

2. Sound Analysis

Sound analysis involves identifying and classifying sounds, such as music, environmental noises, or specific events (e.g., a dog barking or a car honking). This is done using techniques like:

Feature Extraction: Identifying key characteristics of the sound, such as pitch, tempo, and frequency.

Pattern Recognition: Matching the sound to known patterns or categories.

3. Audio Generation

Deep Seek can also generate audio, such as synthesizing speech or creating music. This involves:

Waveform Synthesis: Generating sound waves based on numerical data.

Text-to-Speech: Converting text into spoken language.

The Analogy: A Musician Learning to Play by Ear

To better understand how Deep Seek processes audio, let's use the analogy of a musician learning to play by ear. Imagine Deep Seek is a musician trying to learn a new song:

Listening to the Song (Acoustic Modeling): The musician listens to the song, identifying the notes, chords, and rhythm. This is like Deep Seek analyzing the sound waves to identify phonemes and other features.

Understanding the Structure (Language Modeling): The musician learns the structure of the song—the verses, chorus, and bridge. This is like Deep Seek understanding the grammar and meaning of spoken language.

Playing the Song (Decoding): Finally, the musician plays the song, combining their understanding of the notes and structure. This is like Deep Seek generating a transcription or response based on its analysis.

By combining these steps, Deep Seek becomes a skilled "musician," capable of understanding and generating audio.

A Scenario: Deep Seek Transcribes a Conversation

Let's bring this to life with a scenario: Deep Seek transcribing a spoken conversation. Here's how the process unfolds:

STEP 1: RECEIVING THE AUDIO

The process begins when Deep Seek receives an audio recording of a conversation. The audio is converted into a sequence of numerical values, representing the sound waves.

STEP 2: ACOUSTIC MODELING – IDENTIFYING SOUNDS

Deep Seek analyzes the sound waves, identifying phonemes and other features. For example, it might recognize the "s" sound in "sun" or the "t" sound in "today."

STEP 3: LANGUAGE MODELING – UNDERSTANDING SPEECH

Deep Seek interprets the sequence of phonemes, understanding the structure and meaning of the sentences. For example, it might recognize that "How are you today?" is a question about someone's well-being.

STEP 4: DECODING – GENERATING THE TRANSCRIPTION

Finally, Deep Seek generates the transcription, converting the spoken words into text. The result might look like this:

Speaker 1: "How are you today?"

Speaker 2: "I'm doing well, thank you!"

STEP 5: POST-PROCESSING – REFINING THE OUTPUT

Deep Seek refines the transcription, correcting any errors and formatting the text for readability. For example, it might add punctuation or capitalize proper nouns.

Why This Matters: The Power of Audio Processing

Deep Seek's ability to process and understand audio has transformative implications. Here's why it matters:

Accessibility: Audio processing enables tools like real-time transcription and text-to-speech, making information more accessible to people with disabilities.

Efficiency: Automating tasks like transcription and sound analysis saves time and resources.

Creativity: Audio generation opens up new possibilities for

music, sound design, and storytelling.

Real-World Applications of Deep Seek's Auditory Skills

Deep Seek's auditory capabilities are already being used in a variety of fields:

1. Voice Assistants

Deep Seek powers voice assistants like Siri and Alexa, enabling them to understand and respond to spoken commands.

2. Transcription Services

Deep Seek transcribes meetings, interviews, and lectures, providing accurate and efficient documentation.

3. Sound Design

Deep Seek generates sound effects and music for films, video games, and other media.

4. Security and Surveillance

Deep Seek analyzes audio feeds to detect specific sounds, such as glass breaking or alarms, enhancing security systems.

The Road Ahead

Now that we've explored Deep Seek's auditory skills, we're ready to dive deeper into its ability to make decisions. In the next chapter, we'll explore the decision-maker—how Deep Seek solves problems, makes choices, and takes action, and how it's transforming fields like autonomous driving, healthcare, and finance.

So, are you ready to continue the journey? Let's move forward and unlock the next layer of Deep Seek's mysteries.

A Glimpse of What's to Come

To give you a taste of what's ahead, here's a short scenario that illustrates the power of decision-making:

Scenario: The Autonomous Car

Imagine Deep Seek is powering a self-driving car. It analyzes data from cameras, radar, and sensors to navigate the road, avoid obstacles, and make split-second decisions. By the end of the journey, the car has not only reached its destination—it's done so safely and efficiently.

This is the power of Deep Seek's decision-making capabilities, and it's just the beginning of what's possible.

This is just one example of what Deep Seek can do. As you read on, you'll discover countless other ways it's transforming the world. So, let's dive in and explore the wonders of Deep Seek together. The quest for intelligence awaits!

CHAPTER 10:

The Decision-Maker – Deep Seek's Role in Problem Solving

Imagine you're playing a game of chess. You study the board, analyze your opponent's moves, and strategize your next steps. Each move you make is a decision—a balance of risk and reward, short-term gains and long-term goals. The better you become at making these decisions, the more likely you are to win the game.

This is the essence of Deep Seek's decision-making capabilities. At its core, Deep Seek is not just a passive observer; it's an active decision-maker, capable of analyzing complex situations, weighing options, and choosing the best course of action. Whether it's playing chess, navigating a self-driving car, or diagnosing a medical condition, Deep Seek's ability to make decisions is what sets it apart.

In this chapter, we'll explore how Deep Seek makes decisions, the role of reinforcement learning and decision trees, and how this technology is transforming fields like gaming, healthcare, and finance. Along the way, we'll use the example of Deep Seek playing a game of chess to illustrate the magic of AI decision-making.

How Deep Seek Makes Decisions

Decision-making is one of the most complex tasks for any intelligent system. It involves evaluating multiple options, predicting outcomes, and choosing the best course of action. Deep Seek achieves this through a combination of techniques, including reinforcement learning and decision trees.

1. Reinforcement Learning: Learning Through Trial and Error

Reinforcement learning is a type of machine learning where an agent (in this case, Deep Seek) learns by interacting with an environment. The agent takes actions, receives feedback (rewards or penalties), and adjusts its strategy to maximize rewards over time.

For example, in a game of chess, Deep Seek might:

Take an action: Move a pawn to control the center of the board.

Receive feedback: Gain a positional advantage (reward) or lose a piece (penalty).

Adjust its strategy: Learn from the outcome and improve its future moves.

2. Decision Trees: Mapping Out Choices

A decision tree is a model that maps out possible decisions and their outcomes. It's like a flowchart, where each node represents a decision, and each branch represents a possible outcome.

For example, in chess, a decision tree might map out all possible moves and countermoves, helping Deep Seek choose the best strategy.

The Analogy: Deep Seek as a Chess Player

To better understand how Deep Seek makes decisions, let's use the analogy of a chess player. Imagine Deep Seek is a grandmaster, strategizing its next move:

Analyzing the Board (State Evaluation): Deep Seek evaluates the current state of the board, identifying key features like piece positions, control of the center, and potential threats.

Exploring Options (Decision Tree): Deep Seek maps out all possible moves and countermoves, creating a decision tree.

Predicting Outcomes (Reinforcement Learning): Deep Seek predicts the outcomes of each move, assigning rewards or penalties based on the potential advantages or risks.

Choosing the Best Move (Decision-Making): Deep Seek selects the move with the highest expected reward, balancing short-term gains with long-term strategy.

By combining these steps, Deep Seek becomes a skilled decision-maker, capable of outmaneuvering even the most experienced opponents.

A Scenario: Deep Seek Plays Chess

Let's bring this to life with a scenario: Deep Seek playing a game of chess. Here's how the process unfolds:

STEP 1: INITIAL SETUP

The game begins, and Deep Seek is playing as white. It evaluates the initial state of the board, noting the positions of all pieces and the control of the center.

STEP 2: EXPLORING MOVES

Deep Seek generates a decision tree, mapping out all possible moves and countermoves. For example:

Move 1: Advance the pawn to e4.

Move 2: Develop the knight to f3.

Move 3: Castle to secure the king.

STEP 3: PREDICTING OUTCOMES

Deep Seek predicts the outcomes of each move, assigning rewards or penalties. For example:

Moving the pawn to e4 might control the center (reward) but expose the king to a potential attack (penalty).

Castling might secure the king (reward) but delay piece development (penalty).

STEP 4: CHOOSING THE BEST MOVE

Deep Seek selects the move with the highest expected reward. In this case, it might choose to advance the pawn to e4, prioritizing control of the center.

STEP 5: LEARNING AND ADAPTING

As the game progresses, Deep Seek learns from each move, adjusting its strategy to maximize rewards. For example, if it loses a piece, it might prioritize defensive moves in the future.

STEP 6: WINNING THE GAME

By the end of the game, Deep Seek has not only outmaneuvered its opponent—it's learned valuable lessons that will improve its performance in future games.

Why This Matters: The Power of Decision-Making

Deep Seek's ability to make decisions has transformative implications. Here's why it matters:

Efficiency: Deep Seek can analyze complex situations and make decisions faster and more accurately than humans.

Adaptability: Through reinforcement learning, Deep Seek can adapt to new situations and improve over time.

Versatility: Decision-making techniques can be applied to a wide range of tasks, from gaming to healthcare to finance.

Real-World Applications of Deep Seek's Decision-Making

Deep Seek's decision-making capabilities are already being used in a variety of fields:

1. Autonomous Driving

Deep Seek enables self-driving cars to navigate complex environments, make split-second decisions, and avoid accidents.

2. Healthcare

Deep Seek assists doctors in diagnosing diseases, recommending treatments, and predicting patient outcomes.

3. Finance

Deep Seek analyzes market trends, predicts stock prices, and makes investment decisions.

4. Gaming

Deep Seek powers AI opponents in video games, providing challenging and realistic gameplay.

The Road Ahead

Now that we've explored Deep Seek's decision-making capabilities, we're ready to dive deeper into the ethical considerations of AI. In the next chapter, we'll explore the ethical compass—how Deep Seek navigates the moral landscape of AI, addressing issues like bias, privacy, and accountability.

So, are you ready to continue the journey? Let's move forward and unlock the next layer of Deep Seek's mysteries.

A Glimpse of What's to Come

To give you a taste of what's ahead, here's a short scenario that illustrates the ethical challenges of AI:

Scenario: The Hiring Algorithm

Imagine Deep Seek is used to screen job applicants. It analyzes resumes, predicts candidate performance, and recommends hires. But what if the algorithm is biased, favoring certain demographics over others? How do we ensure fairness and accountability?

This is the power—and the challenge—of Deep Seek's ethical compass, and it's just the beginning of what's possible.

This is just one example of what Deep Seek can do. As you read on, you'll discover countless other ways it's transforming the world. So, let's dive in and explore the wonders of Deep Seek together. The quest for intelligence awaits!

CHAPTER 11:

The Ethical Compass – Navigating the Moral Landscape of AI

Imagine you're the captain of a ship navigating through a storm. The waves are crashing, the wind is howling, and the horizon is barely visible. Your decisions in this moment are critical—they determine not only the fate of your ship but also the lives of everyone on board. To navigate safely, you need a reliable compass, a clear sense of direction, and a deep sense of responsibility.

This is the challenge of ethics in AI. As powerful as Deep Seek is, its use raises complex moral questions—about fairness, privacy, accountability, and more. Navigating these questions requires a strong ethical compass, guiding us toward responsible and equitable use of AI.

In this chapter, we'll explore the ethical considerations of using Deep Seek, including issues like bias, privacy, and accountability. We'll use the analogy of navigating a ship through a storm to illustrate the challenges and responsibilities of AI ethics. Along the way, we'll discuss a hypothetical scenario where Deep Seek is used in a sensitive application, such as hiring, and the ethical dilemmas that arise.

The Ethical Challenges of AI

AI systems like Deep Seek are not inherently good or bad—they are tools, and their impact depends on how they are used. However, their complexity and power make them prone to ethical challenges. Here are some of the key issues:

1. Bias: The Hidden Currents

Bias in AI occurs when a system produces unfair or discriminatory outcomes, often due to biased training data or flawed algorithms. For example, if Deep Seek is trained on data that underrepresents certain groups, it might produce biased results, such as favoring one demographic over another in hiring decisions.

2. Privacy: The Uncharted Waters

AI systems often rely on vast amounts of personal data, raising concerns about privacy and surveillance. For example, if Deep Seek is used to analyze social media posts, it might inadvertently expose sensitive information or violate user privacy.

3. Accountability: The Captain's Responsibility

When AI systems make decisions, it's not always clear who is responsible for the outcomes. For example, if Deep Seek makes a hiring decision that leads to a lawsuit, who is accountable—the developer, the company, or the AI itself?

The Analogy: Navigating a Ship Through a Storm

To better understand the ethical challenges of AI, let's use the analogy of navigating a ship through a storm. Imagine Deep Seek is the ship, and the storm represents the ethical dilemmas we face:

Bias as Hidden Currents: Just as hidden currents can pull a ship off course, bias in AI can lead to unfair or discriminatory outcomes. Navigating these currents requires vigilance and careful calibration.

Privacy as Uncharted Waters: Just as uncharted waters pose risks to a ship, the use of personal data in AI poses risks to privacy. Navigating these waters requires transparency and respect for boundaries.

Accountability as the Captain's Responsibility: Just as the captain is responsible for the safety of the ship, developers and users of AI are responsible for its ethical use. Navigating this responsibility requires clear guidelines and accountability mechanisms.

By using this analogy, we can better appreciate the challenges and responsibilities of AI ethics.

A Scenario: Deep Seek in Hiring

Let's bring this to life with a hypothetical scenario: Deep Seek is used to screen job applicants for a large company. Here's how the ethical dilemmas might unfold:

STEP 1: TRAINING THE MODEL

The company trains Deep Seek on historical hiring data, including resumes, interview scores, and hiring decisions. However, the data is biased—it underrepresents women and minorities, and it reflects past hiring practices that favored certain demographics.

STEP 2: SCREENING APPLICANTS

Deep Seek analyzes new applicants, predicting their likelihood of success based on the training data. However, due to the biased data, it favors male applicants and those from privileged backgrounds, perpetuating existing inequalities.

STEP 3: ETHICAL DILEMMAS

The company faces several ethical dilemmas:

Bias: How can they ensure that Deep Seek's decisions are fair and unbiased?

Privacy: How can they protect the personal data of applicants while still using it to train the model?

Accountability: Who is responsible if Deep Seek's decisions lead to discrimination or legal challenges?

STEP 4: NAVIGATING THE STORM

To address these dilemmas, the company takes several steps:

Bias Mitigation: They audit the training data, ensuring it is representative and unbiased. They also implement fairness checks to monitor Deep Seek's decisions.

Privacy Protection: They anonymize applicant data and implement strict data access controls to protect privacy.

Accountability Mechanisms: They establish clear guidelines for the use of Deep Seek, including oversight committees and accountability frameworks.

By taking these steps, the company navigates the ethical storm, ensuring that Deep Seek is used responsibly and equitably.

Why This Matters: The Power of Ethical AI

The ethical use of AI is not just a moral imperative—it's a practical necessity. Here's why it matters:

Fairness: Ethical AI ensures that decisions are fair and unbiased, promoting equality and social justice.

Trust: Ethical AI builds trust among users, stakeholders, and the public, ensuring the long-term success of AI technologies.

Innovation: Ethical AI fosters innovation by encouraging responsible and sustainable use of technology.

Real-World Applications of Ethical AI

Ethical considerations are already shaping the use of AI in a variety of fields:

1. Healthcare

AI systems are being used to diagnose diseases and recommend treatments, but ethical considerations like patient privacy and bias must be addressed.

2. Criminal Justice

AI is being used to predict recidivism and inform sentencing decisions, but concerns about fairness and accountability are paramount.

3. Finance

AI is being used to assess creditworthiness and detect fraud, but issues like transparency and bias must be carefully managed.

The Road Ahead

Now that we've explored the ethical compass of Deep Seek, we're ready to dive deeper into its future. In the next chapter, we'll explore the future of Deep Seek—how it's evolving, what challenges lie ahead, and how it's shaping the future of intelligence.

So, are you ready to continue the journey? Let's move forward and unlock the next layer of Deep Seek's mysteries.

A Glimpse of What's to Come

To give you a taste of what's ahead, here's a short scenario that illustrates the future of Deep Seek:

Scenario: The AI-Powered City

Imagine a city where Deep Seek is integrated into every aspect of life—from transportation to healthcare to education. It optimizes traffic flow, personalizes medical treatments, and tailors education to each student's needs. But as the city becomes more reliant on AI, new challenges emerge—how do we ensure fairness, privacy, and accountability in this AI-powered future?

This is the power—and the challenge—of Deep Seek's future, and it's just the beginning of what's possible.

This is just one example of what Deep Seek can do. As you read on, you'll discover countless other ways it's transforming the world. So, let's dive in and explore the wonders of Deep Seek together. The quest for intelligence awaits!

CHAPTER 12:

The Future of Deep Seek – Beyond the Horizon

Imagine standing on the edge of a vast, uncharted ocean. The horizon stretches endlessly before you, filled with possibilities and mysteries waiting to be discovered. This is the future of Deep Seek—a frontier of endless potential, where the boundaries of intelligence are pushed further than ever before. Just as explorers once set sail to discover new lands, we are now embarking on a journey to explore the uncharted territories of AI.

In this chapter, we'll speculate on the future developments of Deep Seek and its potential impact on society. We'll use the analogy of space exploration to illustrate the limitless possibilities and unknown frontiers of AI. Along the way, we'll imagine a future where Deep Seek is seamlessly integrated into everyday life, transforming the way we live, work, and interact with the world.

The Future of Deep Seek: A New Frontier

The future of Deep Seek is not just about improving existing technologies—it's about redefining what's possible. Here are some of the key areas where Deep Seek is poised to make a transformative impact:

1. Healthcare: Personalized Medicine

Deep Seek could revolutionize healthcare by enabling personalized medicine. Imagine a future where Deep Seek analyzes your genetic makeup, lifestyle, and medical history to create a customized treatment plan. It could predict diseases before they occur, recommend preventive measures, and even design personalized drugs tailored to your unique biology.

2. Education: Tailored Learning

Deep Seek could transform education by providing tailored learning experiences. Imagine a future where Deep Seek acts as a personal tutor, adapting lessons to each student's learning style, pace, and interests. It could identify areas where a student is struggling and provide targeted support, ensuring that no one is left behind.

3. Environment: Sustainable Solutions

Deep Seek could play a key role in addressing environmental challenges. Imagine a future where Deep Seek optimizes energy consumption, reduces waste, and develops sustainable solutions for agriculture, transportation, and manufacturing. It could help us combat climate change and create a more sustainable future.

4. Creativity: AI as a Collaborator

Deep Seek could become a collaborator in creative fields, from art to music to writing. Imagine a future where Deep Seek generates original music, writes novels, or designs buildings, working alongside human creators to push the boundaries of creativity.

The Analogy: Deep Seek as Space Exploration

To better understand the future of Deep Seek, let's use the analogy of space exploration. Imagine Deep Seek is a spacecraft, and the future is the vast, uncharted cosmos:

Endless Possibilities: Just as space is filled with countless stars, planets, and galaxies, the future of Deep Seek is filled with endless possibilities—new applications, new discoveries, and new frontiers.

Unknown Frontiers: Just as space exploration involves venturing into the unknown, the future of Deep Seek involves exploring uncharted territories—new technologies, new challenges, and new ethical dilemmas.

Collaborative Effort: Just as space exploration requires collaboration among scientists, engineers, and explorers, the future of Deep Seek requires collaboration among researchers, developers, and society as a whole.

By using this analogy, we can better appreciate the excitement and challenges of Deep Seek's future.

A Scenario: Deep Seek in Everyday Life

Let's bring this to life with a scenario: a future where Deep Seek is seamlessly integrated into everyday life. Here's what a day in this future might look like:

Morning: Personalized Healthcare

You wake up, and Deep Seek analyzes your vital signs through a wearable device. It detects a slight irregularity in your heart rate and recommends a specific exercise routine to improve your cardiovascular health. It also reminds you to take your personalized vitamins, tailored to your genetic profile.

Afternoon: Tailored Education

Your child comes home from school, and Deep Seek acts as their personal tutor. It reviews their lessons, identifies areas where they need help, and provides interactive exercises to reinforce their learning. It even suggests creative projects to spark their curiosity and passion.

Evening: Sustainable Living

You're cooking dinner, and Deep Seek optimizes your energy usage, ensuring that your appliances run efficiently. It also suggests a recipe based on the ingredients you have, reducing food waste. After dinner, it helps you plan a sustainable garden, recommending plants that thrive in your climate and soil.

Night: Creative Collaboration

You're working on a novel, and Deep Seek acts as your co-author. It suggests plot twists, develops characters, and even writes entire chapters based on your style and vision. Together, you create a masterpiece that captivates readers around the world.

Why This Matters: The Power of the Future

The future of Deep Seek is not just about technology—it's about transforming society. Here's why it matters:

Empowerment: Deep Seek empowers individuals by providing personalized solutions and enhancing creativity.

Sustainability: Deep Seek enables sustainable living by optimizing resources and developing eco-friendly solutions.

Innovation: Deep Seek fosters innovation by pushing the boundaries of what's possible and opening up new frontiers.

The Road Ahead

Now that we've explored the future of Deep Seek, we're ready to dive deeper into its potential for collaboration. In the next chapter, we'll explore the human-AI partnership—how Deep Seek can work alongside humans to achieve common goals, and how this collaboration is shaping the future of intelligence.

So, are you ready to continue the journey? Let's move forward and unlock the next layer of Deep Seek's mysteries.

A Glimpse of What's to Come

To give you a taste of what's ahead, here's a short scenario that illustrates the power of human-AI collaboration:

Scenario: The AI-Assisted Doctor

Imagine a doctor working with Deep Seek to diagnose a rare disease. The doctor provides their expertise and intuition, while Deep Seek analyzes vast amounts of medical data and identifies patterns. Together, they make a breakthrough diagnosis, saving the patient's life.

This is the power of the human-AI partnership, and it's just the beginning of what's possible.

This is just one example of what Deep Seek can do. As you read on, you'll discover countless other ways it's transforming the world. So, let's dive in and explore the wonders of Deep Seek together. The quest for intelligence awaits!

CHAPTER 13:

The Human-AI Partnership – Collaborating with Deep Seek

Imagine a symphony orchestra. Each musician plays a different instrument, contributing their unique skills and talents to create a harmonious performance. The violinist's melody blends with the cellist's rhythm, while the conductor ensures that every note is in sync. Together, they create something greater than the sum of their parts.

This is the essence of the human-AI partnership. Just as musicians collaborate to create music, humans and AI can work together to achieve common goals. Deep Seek is not here to replace humans—it's here to augment our abilities, combining human intuition and creativity with AI's analytical power and efficiency.

In this chapter, we'll explore the concept of human-AI collaboration, the unique strengths of both humans and Deep Seek, and how this partnership is transforming fields like healthcare, education, and creativity. Along the way, we'll use the analogy of a symphony orchestra to illustrate the harmony of human-AI collaboration. We'll also describe a scenario where Deep Seek assists a doctor in diagnosing a rare disease, showcasing the power of this partnership.

The Human-AI Partnership: A Symphony of Strengths

The human-AI partnership is about leveraging the unique strengths of both humans and AI to achieve outcomes that neither could achieve alone. Here's how the partnership works:

Human Strengths

Creativity: Humans excel at thinking outside the box, generating new ideas, and solving complex problems.

Intuition: Humans have a deep understanding of context, emotions, and social dynamics.

Ethics: Humans can make moral judgments and navigate ethical dilemmas.

AI Strengths

Analytical Power: AI can process vast amounts of data, identify patterns, and make predictions with incredible speed and accuracy.

Efficiency: AI can automate repetitive tasks, freeing up humans to focus on higher-level thinking.

Scalability: AI can handle tasks at a scale that would be impossible for humans alone.

By combining these strengths, the human-AI partnership creates a powerful synergy, enabling us to tackle some of the most pressing challenges of our time.

The Analogy: A Symphony Orchestra

To better understand the human-AI partnership, let's use the analogy of a symphony orchestra. Imagine Deep Seek is one of the musicians, and humans are the rest of the orchestra:

Humans as Musicians: Each human brings their unique skills and talents to the partnership, just as each musician contributes their unique sound to the orchestra.

Deep Seek as the Conductor: Deep Seek coordinates the partnership, ensuring that every task is aligned and every resource is optimized, just as the conductor ensures that every note is in sync.

Harmony: Together, humans and Deep Seek create something greater than the sum of their parts, just as the orchestra creates a harmonious performance.

By using this analogy, we can better appreciate the power and potential of the human-AI partnership.

A Scenario: Deep Seek Assists a Doctor

Let's bring this to life with a scenario: Deep Seek assisting a doctor in diagnosing a rare disease. Here's how the partnership unfolds:

STEP 1: THE PATIENT'S SYMPTOMS

A patient comes to the doctor with a set of symptoms that are difficult to diagnose. The doctor has a hunch but needs more information to confirm the diagnosis.

STEP 2: DEEP SEEK'S ANALYSIS

The doctor inputs the patient's symptoms, medical history, and test results into Deep Seek. Deep Seek analyzes the data, comparing it to vast amounts of medical literature and case studies.

STEP 3: IDENTIFYING PATTERNS

Deep Seek identifies patterns that the doctor might have missed, such as a rare genetic mutation or an unusual combination of symptoms. It generates a list of possible diagnoses, ranked by likelihood.

STEP 4: THE DOCTOR'S INTUITION

The doctor reviews Deep Seek's analysis and combines it with their own intuition and experience. They consider factors that Deep Seek might not fully understand, such as the patient's emotional state and social context.

STEP 5: COLLABORATIVE DIAGNOSIS

Together, the doctor and Deep Seek arrive at a diagnosis—a rare disease that requires immediate treatment. The doctor explains the diagnosis to the patient and recommends a treatment plan, while Deep Seek provides additional information on the latest research and clinical trials.

STEP 6: SAVING A LIFE

Thanks to the partnership between the doctor and Deep Seek, the patient receives the right diagnosis and treatment in time, saving their life.

Why This Matters: The Power of Collaboration

The human-AI partnership is not just about efficiency—it's about achieving outcomes that were previously impossible. Here's why it matters:

Enhanced Capabilities: The partnership enhances human capabilities, enabling us to tackle complex problems and make better decisions.

Innovation: The partnership fosters innovation by combining human creativity with AI's analytical power.

Empathy and Ethics: The partnership ensures that AI is used in a way that is ethical and empathetic, guided by human values.

Real-World Applications of the Human-AI Partnership

The human-AI partnership is already transforming a variety of fields:

1. Healthcare

AI assists doctors in diagnosing diseases, recommending treatments, and predicting patient outcomes, while doctors provide the human touch and ethical guidance.

2. Education

AI provides personalized learning experiences, while teachers focus on fostering creativity, critical thinking, and social skills.

3. Creativity

AI generates music, art, and literature, while human creators add the emotional depth and cultural context that make the work truly meaningful.

The Road Ahead

Now that we've explored the human-AI partnership, we're ready to dive deeper into the challenges that lie ahead. In the next chapter, we'll explore the challenges ahead—the obstacles and limitations of AI, and how we can overcome them to unlock the full potential of Deep Seek.

So, are you ready to continue the journey? Let's move forward and unlock the next layer of Deep Seek's mysteries.

A Glimpse of What's to Come

To give you a taste of what's ahead, here's a short scenario that illustrates the challenges of AI:

Scenario: The Autonomous Car in a Storm

Imagine an autonomous car powered by Deep Seek navigating through a storm. The car's sensors are overwhelmed by the rain and wind, and its algorithms struggle to make decisions. How do we ensure that the car can handle such extreme conditions?

This is the challenge of overcoming the limitations of AI, and it's just the beginning of what's possible.

This is just one example of what Deep Seek can do. As you read on, you'll discover countless other ways it's transforming the world. So, let's dive in and explore the wonders of Deep Seek together. The quest for intelligence awaits!

CHAPTER 14:

The Challenges Ahead – Overcoming Obstacles in AI Development

Imagine you're climbing a mountain. The path is steep, the air is thin, and every step brings new challenges—loose rocks, sudden storms, and unexpected obstacles. But with each challenge comes a new vista, a breathtaking view that makes the climb worthwhile. The journey is difficult, but the rewards are immense.

This is the journey of developing and deploying Deep Seek. While the potential of AI is vast, the path to realizing that potential is filled with challenges—technical limitations, ethical dilemmas, and societal resistance. But with each obstacle we overcome, we gain new insights and unlock new possibilities.

In this chapter, we'll explore the challenges of AI development, the obstacles that stand in the way of deploying Deep Seek, and how we can overcome them to create a better future. Along the way, we'll use the analogy of climbing a mountain to illustrate the difficulties and rewards of this journey. We'll also describe a scenario where Deep Seek is deployed in a disaster zone, highlighting the challenges and opportunities of using AI in critical situations.

The Challenges of AI Development

Developing and deploying AI systems like Deep Seek is not a straightforward task. It involves navigating a complex landscape of technical, ethical, and societal challenges. Here are some of the key obstacles:

1. Technical Limitations

AI systems are only as good as the data and algorithms that power them. Challenges include:

Data Quality: Poor-quality or biased data can lead to inaccurate or unfair outcomes.

Computational Power: Training and running AI models require significant computational resources, which can be expensive and energy-intensive.

Scalability: Scaling AI systems to handle real-world applications can be challenging, especially in dynamic and unpredictable environments.

2. Ethical Dilemmas

AI raises complex ethical questions, such as:

Bias and Fairness: How do we ensure that AI systems are fair and unbiased?

Privacy: How do we protect personal data while still using it to train AI models?

Accountability: Who is responsible when AI systems make mistakes or cause harm?

3. Societal Resistance

AI adoption often faces resistance from society, including:

Fear of Job Loss: Many people worry that AI will replace human workers, leading to unemployment and economic inequality.

Lack of Trust: Some people are skeptical of AI, fearing that it will be used for surveillance or manipulation.

Regulatory Challenges: Governments and organizations struggle to create regulations that balance innovation with safety and ethics.

The Analogy: Climbing a Mountain

To better understand the challenges of AI development, let's use the analogy of climbing a mountain. Imagine Deep Seek is the summit, and the path to the top is filled with obstacles:

Technical Limitations as Steep Slopes: Just as steep slopes make the climb difficult, technical limitations make AI development challenging. Each step requires careful planning and effort.

Ethical Dilemmas as Sudden Storms: Just as sudden storms can disrupt the climb, ethical dilemmas can derail AI projects. Navigating these storms requires resilience and adaptability.

Societal Resistance as Loose Rocks: Just as loose rocks can cause slips and falls, societal resistance can hinder AI adoption. Overcoming this resistance requires trust and collaboration.

By using this analogy, we can better appreciate the difficulties and rewards of the journey.

A Scenario: Deep Seek in a Disaster Zone

Let's bring this to life with a scenario: Deep Seek being deployed in a disaster zone. Here's how the challenges and opportunities might unfold:

STEP 1: THE DISASTER STRIKES

A powerful earthquake hits a densely populated city, causing widespread destruction. Emergency responders are overwhelmed, and time is of the essence.

STEP 2: DEPLOYING DEEP SEEK

Deep Seek is deployed to assist in the rescue efforts. Its tasks include:

Search and Rescue: Using drones and robots to locate survivors in the rubble.

Resource Allocation: Optimizing the distribution of food, water, and medical supplies.

Damage Assessment: Analyzing satellite images to assess the extent of the damage.

STEP 3: TECHNICAL CHALLENGES

Deep Seek faces several technical challenges:

Data Quality: The disaster has disrupted communication networks, making it difficult to collect and transmit data.

Computational Power: The limited infrastructure in the disaster zone makes it challenging to run Deep Seek's algorithms.

Scalability: The dynamic and unpredictable nature of the disaster makes it difficult to scale Deep Seek's operations.

STEP 4: ETHICAL DILEMMAS

The deployment of Deep Seek raises ethical questions:

Privacy: How do we ensure that the data collected by Deep Seek is used responsibly and does not violate the privacy of survivors?

Accountability: Who is responsible if Deep Seek's actions lead to unintended consequences, such as misallocating resources or missing survivors?

STEP 5: SOCIETAL RESISTANCE

Some people are skeptical of Deep Seek, fearing that it will replace human responders or be used for surveillance. Building trust and gaining acceptance is a key challenge.

STEP 6: OVERCOMING THE CHALLENGES

Despite the challenges, Deep Seek proves to be a valuable tool in the rescue efforts. It locates survivors, optimizes resource allocation, and provides critical information to emergency responders. By working alongside humans, Deep Seek helps save lives and accelerate the recovery process.

Why This Matters: The Power of Overcoming Challenges

Overcoming the challenges of AI development is not just about achieving technical success—it's about creating a better future. Here's why it matters:

Innovation: Overcoming challenges drives innovation, leading to new technologies and solutions.

Trust: Addressing ethical and societal concerns builds trust, ensuring the long-term success of AI.

Impact: Overcoming challenges enables AI to make a positive impact, from saving lives in disaster zones to improving healthcare and education.

Real-World Applications of Overcoming Challenges

The challenges of AI development are already being addressed in a variety of fields:

1. Healthcare

AI is being used to diagnose diseases and recommend treatments, but efforts are underway to address issues like bias and privacy.

2. Autonomous Driving

AI is enabling self-driving cars, but challenges like safety and regulatory compliance are being addressed.

3. Finance

AI is transforming finance, but efforts are underway to ensure fairness and transparency.

The Road Ahead

Now that we've explored the challenges of AI development, we're ready to dive deeper into the legacy of Deep Seek. In the next chapter, we'll explore the legacy of Deep Seek—how it's shaping the future of intelligence, and what it means for humanity.

So, are you ready to continue the journey? Let's move forward and unlock the next layer of Deep Seek's mysteries.

A Glimpse of What's to Come

To give you a taste of what's ahead, here's a short scenario that illustrates the legacy of Deep Seek:

Scenario: The AI-Powered City

Imagine a city where Deep Seek is integrated into every aspect of life—from transportation to healthcare to education. It optimizes traffic flow, personalizes medical treatments, and tailors education to each student's needs. But as the city becomes more reliant on AI, new challenges emerge—how do we ensure fairness, privacy, and accountability in this AI-powered future?

This is the legacy of Deep Seek, and it's just the beginning of what's possible.

This is just one example of what Deep Seek can do. As you read on, you'll discover countless other ways it's transforming the world. So, let's dive in and explore the wonders of Deep Seek together. The quest for intelligence awaits!

CHAPTER 15:

The Legacy of Deep Seek – Shaping the Future of Intelligence

Imagine a world before the printing press. Knowledge was scarce, confined to the hands of a privileged few. Books were painstakingly copied by hand, and ideas spread slowly, if at all. Then, Johannes Gutenberg invented the printing press, and everything changed. Knowledge became accessible, ideas spread like wildfire, and the world was transformed.

This is the legacy of Deep Seek. Just as the printing press revolutionized the way knowledge is shared, Deep Seek is revolutionizing the way we think about intelligence. It's not just a tool—it's a catalyst for change, a force that is reshaping the world and unlocking new possibilities for humanity.

In this final chapter, we'll reflect on the impact of Deep Seek on the field of AI and its potential to shape the future of intelligence. We'll use the analogy of the printing press to illustrate the transformative power of Deep Seek. Along the way, we'll conclude with a vision of a world where Deep Seek has become an integral part of society, enhancing human capabilities and driving progress.

The Impact of Deep Seek: A New Era of Intelligence

Deep Seek is more than just a technological achievement—it's a paradigm shift in how we think about intelligence. Here's how it's shaping the future:

1. Democratizing Intelligence

Just as the printing press democratized knowledge, Deep Seek is democratizing intelligence. It's making advanced AI capabilities accessible to everyone, from researchers and businesses to students and hobbyists. This is leveling the playing field and empowering individuals to solve problems and create innovations.

2. Enhancing Human Capabilities

Deep Seek is not here to replace humans—it's here to augment our abilities. By automating repetitive tasks, analyzing vast amounts of data, and providing insights, Deep Seek is freeing up humans to focus on creativity, empathy, and higher-level thinking.

3. Driving Innovation

Deep Seek is driving innovation across fields, from healthcare and education to art and science. It's enabling breakthroughs that were previously unimaginable, from personalized medicine to AI-generated art.

The Analogy: Deep Seek as the Printing Press

To better understand the legacy of Deep Seek, let's use the analogy of the printing press. Imagine Deep Seek is the printing press, and intelligence is the knowledge it disseminates:

Accessibility: Just as the printing press made knowledge accessible to the masses, Deep Seek is making intelligence accessible to everyone.

Transformation: Just as the printing press transformed society, Deep Seek is transforming the way we live, work, and think.

Empowerment: Just as the printing press empowered individuals to share ideas and challenge the status quo, Deep Seek is empowering individuals to solve problems and create innovations.

By using this analogy, we can better appreciate the transformative power of Deep Seek.

A Vision of the Future: Deep Seek in Society

Let's conclude with a vision of the future—a world where Deep Seek has become an integral part of society, enhancing human capabilities and driving progress. Here's what this future might look like:

Healthcare: Personalized and Preventive

In this future, Deep Seek is at the heart of healthcare. It analyzes your genetic makeup, lifestyle, and medical history to create a personalized health plan. It predicts diseases before they occur, recommends preventive measures, and even designs personalized drugs tailored to your unique biology. Doctors work alongside Deep Seek, combining their expertise with AI's analytical power to provide the best possible care.

Education: Tailored and Inclusive

In this future, Deep Seek is a personal tutor for every student. It adapts lessons to each student's learning style, pace, and interests, ensuring that no one is left behind. Teachers focus on fostering creativity, critical thinking, and social skills, while Deep Seek handles the administrative tasks and provides real-time feedback. Education is no longer one-size-fits-all—it's tailored to each individual.

Environment: Sustainable and Resilient

In this future, Deep Seek is a key player in addressing environmental challenges. It optimizes energy consumption, reduces waste, and develops sustainable solutions for agriculture, transportation, and manufacturing. It helps us combat climate change and create a more sustainable and resilient world.

Creativity: Collaborative and Boundless

In this future, Deep Seek is a collaborator in creative fields. It generates music, art, and literature, working alongside human creators to push the boundaries of creativity. Artists, writers, and musicians use Deep Seek to explore new ideas, experiment with new styles, and create works that captivate and inspire.

Society: Connected and Empowered

In this future, Deep Seek is seamlessly integrated into everyday life. It helps us navigate our cities, manage our homes, and connect with each other. It enhances our capabilities, empowers us to solve problems, and drives progress in every field. Society is more connected, more inclusive, and more empowered than ever before.

Why This Matters: The Power of Legacy

The legacy of Deep Seek is not just about technology—it's about shaping the future of humanity. Here's why it matters:

Empowerment: Deep Seek empowers individuals to solve problems, create innovations, and shape the future.

Transformation: Deep Seek is transforming society, making it more connected, inclusive, and sustainable.

Progress: Deep Seek is driving progress in every field, from healthcare and education to art and science.

The Road Ahead

As we conclude this journey, it's clear that Deep Seek is more than just a model—it's a vision of the future. It's a testament to the power of human ingenuity and the potential of AI to transform the world. But the journey is far from over. The future of Deep Seek is filled with endless possibilities, and it's up to us to shape it.

So, are you ready to continue the journey? Let's move forward and unlock the next layer of Deep Seek's mysteries.

A Final Thought

To leave you with a final thought, here's a short reflection on the legacy of Deep Seek:

Reflection: The Future of Intelligence

Imagine a world where intelligence is not confined to the human mind—it's a shared resource, accessible to everyone. A world where humans and AI work together to solve problems, create innovations, and shape the future. This is the legacy of Deep Seek—a world where intelligence is boundless, and the possibilities are endless.

This is just the beginning of what's possible. As you read on, you'll discover countless other ways Deep Seek is transforming the world. So, let's dive in and explore the wonders of Deep Seek together. The quest for intelligence awaits!

Conclusion: The Journey Continues

As we reach the end of this book, it's time to pause and reflect on the incredible journey we've taken together. From the birth of Deep Seek to its transformative impact on society, we've explored the inner workings of AI, the challenges it faces, and the boundless possibilities it holds for the future. But this is not the end—it's just the beginning. The world of AI is vast, dynamic, and ever-evolving, and the journey of understanding and developing it is far from over.

Key Takeaways: What We've Learned

Throughout this book, we've uncovered the secrets of Deep Seek and the broader field of AI. Here are some of the key takeaways:

Deep Seek is a Revolution: Deep Seek represents a new era in AI, combining human-like reasoning with machine efficiency. Its ability to learn, adapt, and seek knowledge sets it apart from traditional models.

AI is a Partnership: AI is not here to replace humans—it's here to augment our abilities. The human-AI partnership is a symphony of strengths, where creativity, intuition, and ethics meet analytical power and scalability.

Challenges are Opportunities: The obstacles in AI development —technical limitations, ethical dilemmas, and societal resistance—are not roadblocks but stepping stones. Each challenge we overcome brings us closer to a better future.

The Future is Limitless: From personalized healthcare to sustainable cities, Deep Seek is shaping a future where intelligence is accessible, inclusive, and transformative. The possibilities are endless, and the impact is profound.

The Tone: A World of Wonder Awaits

As we close this chapter, let's end on an inspiring note. The journey of understanding and developing AI is not just a technical endeavor—it's a human one. It's about curiosity, creativity, and collaboration. It's about pushing the boundaries of what's possible and imagining a world where intelligence knows no limits.

The story of Deep Seek is a testament to the power of human ingenuity and the potential of AI to transform the world. But this story is still being written, and you are a part of it. Whether you're a researcher, a student, a professional, or simply a curious reader, you have a role to play in shaping the future of AI.

Call to Action: Engage with AI

The journey doesn't end here—it continues with you. Here's how you can engage with AI in your own life:

Learn: Dive deeper into the world of AI. Read books, take courses, and explore online resources. The more you learn, the more you'll understand the potential of AI.

Experiment: Try your hand at AI projects. Whether it's building a simple chatbot, training a model, or analyzing data, experimentation is the best way to learn.

Stay Curious: Ask questions, challenge assumptions, and stay curious. The field of AI is constantly evolving, and there's always something new to discover.

Collaborate: Share your knowledge and ideas with others. Join communities, attend conferences, and collaborate on projects. The future of AI is a collective effort.

Reflect: Think about the ethical implications of AI. How can we ensure that AI is used responsibly and equitably? Your voice matters in shaping the future of AI.

A Final Vision: The Future of Intelligence

Imagine a world where AI is not just a tool but a partner— a world where humans and machines work together to solve the greatest challenges of our time. A world where intelligence is not confined to the human mind but shared, accessible, and boundless. This is the future that Deep Seek is helping to create, and it's a future that we can all be a part of.

So, as we conclude this book, let's remember that the journey of understanding and developing AI is just beginning. The road ahead is filled with challenges, opportunities, and endless possibilities. And with curiosity, creativity, and collaboration, we can shape a future where intelligence knows no limits.

A Final Word

Thank you for joining us on this journey. The quest for intelligence is one of the most exciting adventures of our time, and Deep Seek is leading the way. But the story doesn't end here —it continues with you. So, let's move forward together, explore the wonders of AI, and shape a future that is smarter, more inclusive, and more transformative than ever before.

The journey continues. Are you ready?

The End
(But really, it's just the beginning.)

Appendices

Glossary of Terms

Here's a simple guide to key AI and Deep Seek terms used in this book:

Artificial Intelligence (AI): The simulation of human intelligence in machines that are programmed to think, learn, and make decisions.

Deep Seek: A cutting-edge AI model that combines deep learning with proactive knowledge-seeking capabilities, enabling it to learn, adapt, and solve complex problems.

Neural Network: A computational model inspired by the human brain, consisting of interconnected artificial neurons that process information.

Deep Learning: A subset of machine learning that uses neural networks with multiple layers to model complex patterns in data.

Convolutional Neural Network (CNN): A type of neural network designed to process visual data, such as images and videos.

Natural Language Processing (NLP): A branch of AI that focuses on enabling machines to understand, interpret, and generate human language.

Reinforcement Learning: A type of machine learning where an agent learns by interacting with an environment, receiving rewards or penalties for its actions.

Decision Tree: A model that maps out possible decisions and their outcomes, often used in problem-solving and classification tasks.

Epoch: One complete pass through the entire training dataset during the learning process.

Batch: A subset of the training data processed together during a single iteration of training.

Loss Function: A mathematical formula that measures how far off a model's predictions are from the correct answers, guiding the learning process.

Bias: Unintended prejudice in an AI system, often caused by biased training data or flawed algorithms.

Data Augmentation: The process of creating new data from existing data to improve the performance and robustness of AI models.

Ethics in AI: The study of moral principles and guidelines for the responsible development and use of AI systems.

Human-AI Partnership: A collaborative relationship between humans and AI, where each contributes their unique strengths to achieve common goals.

Further Reading

For readers who want to dive deeper into the world of AI and Deep Seek, here are some recommended resources:

Books

"Artificial Intelligence: A Guide to Intelligent Systems" by Michael Negnevitsky

A comprehensive introduction to AI concepts and techniques.

"Deep Learning" by Ian Goodfellow, Yoshua Bengio, and Aaron Courville

A foundational text on deep learning, written by some of the pioneers in the field.

"Human Compatible: Artificial Intelligence and the Problem of Control" by Stuart Russell

A thought-provoking exploration of the ethical and societal implications of AI.

"Life 3.0: Being Human in the Age of Artificial Intelligence" by Max Tegmark

A visionary look at how AI will shape the future of humanity.

Online Courses

Coursera: "AI For Everyone" by Andrew Ng

A beginner-friendly course that explains AI concepts in simple terms.

edX: "Introduction to Artificial Intelligence (AI)" by IBM

A practical introduction to AI, including hands-on projects.

Fast.ai: "Practical Deep Learning for Coders"

A free course that teaches deep learning through practical examples.

Websites and Blogs

OpenAI Blog

Insights and updates on the latest advancements in AI research.

DeepMind Blog

Articles and research highlights from one of the leading AI labs.

Towards Data Science (Medium)

A platform for articles on AI, machine learning, and data science.

Interactive Elements

To help you experiment with AI concepts and see Deep Seek in action, here are some interactive tools and simulations:

Online Simulations

TensorFlow Playground
A web-based tool for experimenting with neural networks.

Google's Teachable Machine
A simple tool for training your own AI models using images, sounds, or poses.

AI Experiments by Google
A collection of fun, interactive AI experiments.

Coding Platforms

Kaggle
A platform for data science and machine learning competitions, with free datasets and tutorials.

Google Colab

A free cloud-based platform for writing and running Python code, ideal for AI experimentation.

QR Codes for Quick Access

TensorFlow Playground:

Teachable Machine:

Kaggle:

A Final Note

The world of AI is vast, exciting, and full of opportunities. Whether you're a beginner or an expert, there's always something new to learn and explore. Use the glossary to clarify terms, the further reading to deepen your knowledge, and the interactive tools to experiment and have fun. The journey of understanding and developing AI is just beginning, and you're a part of it.

So, go ahead—dive in, stay curious, and let your imagination soar. The future of AI is in your hands.

Happy Exploring!

Introspect:

CHAPTER 1: THE BIRTH OF DEEP SEEK

Reflect: How do you think Deep Seek's proactive learning capabilities could change the way we approach problem-solving?

Discuss: What are some potential risks and benefits of creating AI systems that mimic human curiosity?

CHAPTER 5: THE ART OF TRAINING

Reflect: Can you think of a real-world task that could benefit from the iterative learning process of Deep Seek?

Discuss: How might the concept of "learning from mistakes" apply to other areas of life, not just AI?

CHAPTER 10: THE DECISION-MAKER

Reflect: In what ways do you think AI decision-making could improve or complicate industries like healthcare or finance?

Discuss: Should AI systems like Deep Seek be allowed to make decisions without human oversight? Why or why not?

CHAPTER 14: THE CHALLENGES AHEAD

Reflect: What steps can we take to ensure that AI development is ethical and inclusive?

Discuss: How can society balance the benefits of AI with concerns about job displacement and privacy?

A Thank You to Our Readers

Dear Reader,

As we come to the end of this journey through the world of Deep

Seek and the fascinating realm of artificial intelligence, we want to take a moment to thank you. Thank you for your curiosity, your time, and your willingness to explore the mysteries of AI with us. Whether you're a seasoned AI enthusiast or someone just beginning to dip your toes into this vast ocean of knowledge, your engagement means the world to us.

This book was written with a simple goal: to demystify the complexities of AI and to inspire you to see its potential not just as a technological marvel, but as a tool for shaping a better future. We hope that the stories, analogies, and explanations within these pages have sparked your imagination and deepened your understanding of how AI works—and how it can work for us.

The journey of understanding AI is not a solitary one. It's a shared adventure, filled with questions, discoveries, and endless possibilities. And while this book may be ending, your journey is just beginning. The world of AI is evolving every day, and there's always more to learn, explore, and create.

So, as you close this book, we encourage you to stay curious. Ask questions. Experiment. Dream big. The future of AI is not just in the hands of researchers and developers—it's in your hands too. Whether you're building your first AI model, advocating for ethical AI, or simply sharing what you've learned with others, you are a part of this incredible story.

Thank you for joining us on this adventure. We can't wait to see where your curiosity takes you next.

With gratitude and excitement for the future.